wild child

girlhoods

in the

counterculture

edited by
chelsea cain

foreword by
moon zappa

 Seal Press

Seal Press
An Imprint of
Avalon Publishing Group, Inc
1400 65th St., Ste. 250
Emeryville, CA 94608

Cover photograph by Mary Cain
Text design by Maren Costa

Rivka K. Solomon's essay "Thanksgiving '71" first aired on Boston's National Public Radio Station, WBUR.

"Our Mail Truck Days." From *Split: A Counterculture Childhood.* Copyright © 1998 by Lisa Michaels. Reprinted by permission of Houghton Mifflin Company. All rights reserved.

"Canvastown," "Appetites," "Kanji" and "Membrane" by Paola Bilbrough first appeared in *Bell Tongue* © 1999 by Paola Bilbrough, published by Victoria University Press, Wellington, New Zealand.

Photo credits may be found on page 191, which constitutes a continuation of the copyright page.

Library of Congress Cataloging-in-Publication Data
Wild child : girlhoods in the counterculture / edited by Chelsea Cain.
1. Girls—United States—History—20th century.
2. Girls—United States—Biography. 3. Social History—1960–1970.
4. Hippies—United States. 5. United States—History—1961–1969.
I. Cain, Chelsea
HQ777.W55 1999   305.23'0973—dc21   99-044610
ISBN-10: 1-58005-031-X
ISBN-13: 978-1-58005-031-9

Printed in Canada by Transcontinental
First printing, December 1999
10 9 8 7 6 5 4 3 2

Distributed to the trade by Publishers Group West
In Canada: Publishers Group West Canada, Toronto, Ontario
In the U.K. and Europe: Hi Marketing, London, UK
In Australia: Bookwise International, Wingfield, South Australia

For William and Kate Schmidt,
who gave their grandchildren the ocean,
and for all our parents.

Acknowledgments

F irst and foremost, thanks to all the women who contributed to this book. They are a sharp and groovy crew who have given me the gift of their memories, and of their acquaintance. Thanks also to Moon, who graciously agreed to write the foreword and has more cool in her little finger than most people have in their entire bodies. Special thanks to Jennie Goode and everyone at Seal, for their smarts, enthusiasm and endless patience (I'm going to move into the office just as soon as I find a cover for the couch). This book, as with everything I do, is indebted to my mother, Mary Cain, who continues to teach me how to live, and to my dad, for trusting me to live wisely. Also, thanks to my family (the aunts especially, Roddy and Susan D.) and my friends, many of whom read perilous drafts of this book. I am lucky to know such fine and excellent people.

Contents

✶ Foreword

moon zappa

My name is Moon Unit Zappa. I was born in New York City on September 28, 1967. So the story goes, my parents had been married just a handful of days prior to my birth, and as my father was leaving to go on tour for a frightful stretch in support of his latest musical efforts (and us), he gave my mother the option of naming me either Moon Unit or Motorhead. A simple offering of two names to choose between in his absence, having nothing to do with gender. When I arrived she selected Moon.

Were we hippies? My dad *hated* granola and tofu. In fact, he willfully ate Hormel chili from the can and plump-when-you-cook-'em *meat* hot dogs, which he skewered on a fork and cooked over an open gas burner on our kitchen stove, like a home-owning hobo. No one was *Oming* in my house and pachouli and drugs were forbidden. The pure hit of reality was the high we were riding.

Yet we called our parents Frank and Gail (never Mom and

Dad), we were allowed to decide whether or not we felt like going to school on any given day, and later, when we were teenagers, my mother insisted that we shower with our overnight guests in order to conserve water.

We lived in Laurel Canyon. Where all the rock stars were. Where all the artists were. Where all the people who were going to take over the world with their God-given creativity were. My mother smoked cigarettes and ate mostly peanut butter and grapefruit. She didn't wear shoes when she went to the grocery store. She certainly didn't wear a bra. She made English Breakfast tea with milk and sugar for scantily clad women with smudgy eye makeup, women who smelled like powdery old books. The men who visited us had patchy beards and bad posture and smelled like B.O. Crouching in the nude near my playthings, they melted brightly colored crayons and made candles out of old milk cartons. Everyone seemed to be unwashed, musky and recently fucked. If they wore clothes, they were flamboyant, mismatched garments with bright colors and crazy patterns that clashed. On the men, clothing always clung to the fleshy parts of their bodies, and drooped and flared where there was hardly any meat on their bones. The women wore tissue paper–thin kerchiefs or dyed, crocheted, doilyesque halters that left nothing to the imagination. I have a vague memory of women attempting to conceal large areolas with black masking tape and colored Magic Marker.

At my house, clothes were an extension of the imagination, used to name who or what you were for the hour or so you had them on, a dinosaur or a witch or a superhero. Clothes were costumes for putting on shows. When I had to leave the house and go to a place where people might be wearing clothes, my mother let me wear my frilly coocaracha underwear on my head. My hair was wildly unbrushed and I could pull clumps of it out of the leg holes to make ears if I wanted, but mainly my undies were a hat. Once, when my mother (barefoot, of course) hitchhiked to the grocery store with me in tow, a man approached us in the dairy section and tried to sweet-talk me to get to her. At the ripe old age of two, I already knew enough to sense that something was energetically ick about the whole shabooh, and reportedly announced, "Fuck off, pervert."

By the time I was six, I began to notice that my family was different. My first clue was a television show for preschoolers called *Romper Room*. At the close of every show the teacher would look in her magic mirror and say goodbye to the children lucky enough to be named Susan or Kim or Debbie or Michael or Billy. No mention of a Moon Unit or a Dweezil (my brother, two years my junior, with hair and eyelashes longer than my own). Nor did we look like the children on an incomprehensibly dull *Mr. Rogers* or *Sesame Street*. No first-graders I knew found pornographic cartoons lying around next to blow-up sex dolls in their childproof homes with the backyard swingsets. They didn't know about R&B or astrology or the Ouija board or how to have a séance. Absolutely no one my age cussed (and therefore remained sadly unaware of our terrific freedom-of-speech amendment) or knew what gay was or made Barbie and Ken fuck and orgasm loudly or bent spoons in her spare time or got to stay up late and either go to clubs, or watch scary movies or skin flicks with *their* moms and dads. Other children could not keep up with me or keep me entertained; neither could timid grownups for that matter. The most fun I could hope for was to see the look of horror on another child's face, one with the normal parents, as I scared her into awareness, hoping, I now realize, to get a glimpse of what my reaction to what was happening around me was supposed to look like.

Which is why when I first heard about Chelsea's project, I took an immediate interest in the book. The testimonials of children caught between two worlds? Hippie parents combined with obedient, conservative grandparents? The pendulum swing of our parents' chosen lifestyles in sharp, rebellious contrast to the lives their parents chose, and the effects of all this on their lab-rat offspring? Yippee! Throw in a special, soul-sisters-only vibe from the daughters of *the* daughters who courageously said "yes" to living life as the equals of men, in defiance of societal norms and authoritarian opposition, and you have one sa-weet deal. For me, personally, a chance to not feel like a mutant outcast because I get to discover other girl humans who endured some of the same bizarro shit in their households.

It turns out I'm not the only one who grew up with the same regard for everyone and every living thing. Like these ladies, I was taught that no man or woman is above you. Not even a policeman or a president or a pope. I was told these are just jobs. People in the army or the government, or lawyers ... that's just what they do, not who they are. Authority figures? Ha! Underneath their uniforms and beliefs are flesh and blood humans, same as me. We all answer to something larger than ourselves; therefore, the act of simply calling a teacher or a grownup "Miss" or "Mr." seemed like a ridiculous, arbitrary, socially agreed-upon rule for an agreed-upon order. It stirs up the same confusion in me now when I stop for a red light in the middle of the night on a deserted road. (I confess, sometimes I sneak through. But ya better do it while you can, before they implement those evil cameras at *every* corner to monitor our diligence in obeying the rules about when to stop and when to go.) At my house we were exposed to everything, because knowledge is power. At my house there was no supervision, so there was no reason to sneak. At my house there were no rules, so there was nothing to rebel against. I hated it.

It always left me with an awful floating feeling that most, if not all, of these lovelies experienced, of too much space, of too many choices. I felt very often (and still do) like I was doing a moon walk and my cord came loose from the ship. Ick. I craved rituals and rules like my friends had. I prayed for curfews and strictly enforced dinner times. Uniforms and organized events and people with *goals* amazed me.

Before reading this book, I thought of hippies as people who were in tune enough with nature to remember to look up from time to time—to notice the vigilant sun and moon standing as sweet reminders that happiness is always available to us—but not grounded enough to retain and make use of this understanding. Hippies can't be bothered with uptight concepts like good grooming or looking presentable. Hippies take the time to discover "the truth" about Who We All Really Are out in the boonies, safe from society's soul-poisoning distractions, but do not have actual jobs, and whose discoveries are therefore rendered useless and ineffectual to the rest of man(notso)kind. Hippies are either meditating in absolute silence, or in symbiosis with nature and her bountiful herb—eating, growing and smoking organic, but lacking the follow-through to vote or take action to protect all things green. God knows how slowly things run in a health food eatery or co-op checkout line. Hippies explore sexually taboo terrain but their children, too young to choose the lifestyle for themselves, suffer the consequences of being exposed to too much stimulus too early on, more than most of us experience in a lifetime.

I am only half right. After reading this book and the offerings of the women hand-picked by Ms. Cain, I've happily come to new understandings about others and myself. It turns out that I am not as isolated as I once thought. It turns out that I am part of a tribe (of fringies, but a tribe nonetheless). Understanding and accepting fringie life helps me to better navigate the waters of the normie world, for although I am not as crunchy as some, I am certainly crispier than most. I am proud that I, like so many of the women in this book, will never have beige carpeting in my house, will never own or wear a skirt suit, will never revere misogynistic steak-house politics, and will never be a *Rules* girl, obedient to some outdated, fifties model of partnership. I find there is a common bond and an actual language that is immediately understood by super-crunchy-granola types, one that is as colloquially familiar to me as val speak or wall street chic cheek is to its kind. This book explains my envy of the French language with its luxury of a *tu* and *vous* to establish a boundary of familiarity, something that is sorely lacking in my own vocabulary. It unravels the mystery behind late bloomers with my background. As a child, I was given free rein; now I am only employable as an empress of the universe, or something in "the arts." (I *can't* be in fluorescent lighting, it's against my body's religion.) In a love-all-serve-all-blurred-edges-universe, one tends to lose oneself rather easily. Whatever it is I believed hippies lacked in goals, I now realize they more than make up for in tolerance.

Growing up between two worlds, I learned to judge people by their actions, not their outsides. People are either part of the problem or part of the solution. For or against the planet and everyone on it. Black, white, fat, skinny—who cares? The wise counterculture hippie in me doesn't care about that. Lazy is not black or white or brown or yellow. It is lazy. Sexual carelessness is not hippie; it is sexual carelessness. Lastly, everyone has a story to tell, everyone is unique and everyone has to find her own way in this world regardless of her upbringing and her relation to the starting line.

If you grew up in bare feet, you may find this book a comforting balm of commonality. If you are a normie, you might appreciate the, at times, alien differences between us and our collective "life is short but very wide" approach to things. Either way, these essays offer a vivid glimpse of the wild ride of a counterculture childhood. All in all, a compelling anthropological gathering.

Love,
Moon Zappa
August 1999

✯ Introduction

chelsea cain

This is what I remember: the rusted frame of an old car abandoned in a ditch near the farm, Ray sitting on an overturned bucket watching his vegetable garden grow, the comings and goings of men in John Deere caps and plaid shirts to and from the barn across the road, the long drive into town in the red '62 Ford truck, the taste of dust rising from the lane, the blackberries, the smell of wet dogs, standing on my tip toes to pluck a seed from a sunflower, gathering brown eggs in the chicken coop, priming the pump, swimming in the pond, snapping turtles, strawberries, morning glories, snapdragons, the Allman Brothers' *Brothers and Sisters* album cover, how there was music, always music, music during big dinners at the long table in the kitchen, music that colored everything (the kitchen was yellow, the house was white, my dress was red), music at night when the dogs would run barking in a pack through the neighbors' fields, listening to Bob Dylan on the porch while my mother taught me the difference between Chile tomatoes and cherry tomatoes in our garden, waking up every morning to music.

I am the child of hippies. I spent my plump, naked girlhood frolicking through the vegetable garden and spinning on the porch to crazed, hippie banjo music. I called my parents by their first names until I was nine and knew who John Lennon was before I had heard of Jesus Christ. Grace Slick and Che Guevara were my role models—not Farrah Fawcett, not Betty Ford. I wanted to grow up to be a fire dog. I ate millet casserole and wheat bread, uncoerced. I was weaned on goat's milk. Until I was six, I insisted on wearing a different color sock on each foot. I ran with the dogs. I buried my dolls. My mother told me I was an artist. My father taught me to sing. I didn't take baths. I believed Richard Nixon was lying, and I believed I could grow up to do anything.

For my parents and their friends, the idea at the heart of the counterculture was simple: rejection. Rejection of the Establishment's war, its social mores, its institutions, its hang-ups, its corruption and its pantsuits. The counterculture was a social phenomenon, not a political one. There was no hippie manifesto and, unless you count Woodstock, no one ever called a summit meeting. Yet, some common threads linked the hippies. Like my parents, many were from white, middle-class backgrounds. Many were antiwar. Many used drugs. But the hippies were not at the forefront of the anti-Vietnam movement, like the students or other members of the New Left. Their form of social protest was nonparticipation—total rejection of the war machine and all its accouterments. Cops were "pigs," the president was a crook, America was spelled with a "K," adults were not to be trusted—even white sugar was suspect.

Although the hippie trip started out as a social experiment, it became political despite itself. The hippies set about creating a lifestyle that not only abandoned, but defied the cultural norms. By rejecting the expectations and betrayals of their upbringings, they could start fresh with the next generation. They could change the world one child at a time.

Back in the "real" world, the world my parents had forsaken, the questionable futures of these children soon became the source of much anxiety along the cul de sac. What was to become of kids like me who had been denied meat, exposed to free love, and given nouns instead of names? What future lay in store for children who were raised with no boundaries, who knew about drugs and Janis Joplin and the female orgasm, who were never instructed in the art of personal hygiene, who were alienated from mainstream culture, who were taught to question authority, government, the social order? Certainly such children would be ill prepared to participate in "normal" society, much less join the Junior League. At best they would be maladjusted; at worst, sex-addicted, atheist, communist artists.

Hippie kids grew up the products of a great experiment. As with any scene, there were good parents, and bad parents, and everyone's experience was not the same. But these parents were all trying something different, something radical, something revolutionary. Their failures, in many cases, could be considered as unique and interesting as their successes.

What better way to learn about a lifestyle than by looking at the children it produced? How successful were the hippies at insulating themselves from mainstream culture, and what influences could they not escape? How have the children of the hippies taken up their parents' legacy of rebellion? What aspects of the counterculture have these children embraced as adults, and what have they rejected?

As children of the counterculture, we faced constant negotiation between home life and outside influences. We learned to live between two worlds: the one our parents created and the straight one that surrounded us. Our parents couldn't shield us from mainstream culture—though many of them tried. They could simply do their best to pass on their values and beliefs about a difficult, corrupt world. Many of us still struggle with this dichotomy, vainly attempting to be true to each world and betray neither. We may be hippies at home and yuppies in the office. We might want to make pottery and grow organic vegetables and still be drawn to cell phones and Jettas. We struggle to retain the truth of who we are, which many of us find rooted in our childhoods, even as we live in a world that may eschew our alternative beginnings.

Our parents offered us a rare freedom to create our lives as we chose. It was part of a larger commitment to freedom that came to define the hippie counterculture. Free love, free speech, freedom from societal restraints. Those of us who felt safe in this freedom reveled in it, those of us who did not feel safe pined for structure, curfews, limits. Freedom without a safety net can have dire and lasting results. In collecting these stories, I wanted to explore what hippie kids had learned about freedom from coming of age in an environment that valued it so highly yet may not have considered all of its consequences.

I have chosen to focus on girls, because I think that raising a girl "outside" of society has particularly radical implications. These hippie girls were raised in an era that was just beginning to liberate girls from the expectations that accompanied generations of social and sexual repression. They were being raised by young women who had rejected the roles prescribed to them, for the promised liberation of the counterculture. I was interested to see what type of feminism this would spawn. How would that early empowerment affect their gender politics? The writers in this book all have strong independent voices; they are the daughters of mothers who were courageous or desperate enough to walk away from a lifetime of gender roles and boundaries. For many of these women, the promised liberation of the counterculture proved to be an empty one, as traditional gender roles followed them to the communes and the farmhouses. For their daughters, the promise was to prove more fruitful.

I started this project in an effort to understand my own experience, through the experience of my peers. Of my values, beliefs, propensities, quirks—of who I am today—what do I owe to my upbringing, and what is simply a result of my own inevitable peculiarities? Yet, this anthology has taught me much more than that. Its lasting value will not be only in the anecdotal memoirs themselves, but in their collective insight on the unique impact that this specific social experiment had on its children, and how that impact, and its implications on child rearing, has not yet finished reverberating.

This anthology begins with a birth and ends with another. We come full circle, from girl-child to woman to girl-child. To begin, Zoë Eakle writes of her home birth to hippie expatriates on the Canadian island of her childhood. To end, Suzanne M. Cody writes a letter to her infant daughter about her own girlhood, and what she would and would not change. In between, Ariel Gore laments what was lost when the world, the counterculture and her childhood changed. Poet Paola Bilbrough remembers her New Zealand counterculture girlhood in poetry that is evocative of the strange magic particular to her hippie outback home. Elizabeth Shé describes the darker side of free love run amok. For a perspective of another sort, Angela Lam writes not of her own girlhood in the counterculture, but of her friend, Summer, and how a brief encounter with Summer's family challenged Angela's sheltered world. These and the other essays recount a particular American childhood in ways that shed light not just on their parents' choices, but on the radical implications of attempting to raise children outside of mainstream society.

A social experiment only becomes revolutionary when its implications transcend the moment, when it pervades and changes the society, when it ripples through the generations. The legacy of the hippie trip is not merely in its children, but in the fact that we are still working through the lessons of our upbringing, the successes and the failures. What we take from that experience, what we incorporate into our own lives—*that* is the legacy. We are sex-addicted, atheist, communist artists, after all. We are the people our grandparents warned us about. And we are having children. It can only lead to more "uncivilized" behavior.

Our parents laid down their weapons long ago, but the hippie kids in this anthology, and all the hippie kids I know, still struggle with questions: questions like when to take on society, and when to go along; when to live in the straight world, and when to abandon the rat race and take a summer off to follow Phish; when to march against clear-cutting-animal-testing-ozone-destroying-pro-life-legislating-poor-people-exploiting-fundamentalist-special-interests, and when to stay home and watch *The Road Rules* on MTV.

If there is anything that these essays teach us it is this: There is just no way that you can escape being influenced by a childhood designed specifically to influence you. We were raised in a culture intended to teach us to challenge everything everybody else was telling us—to subvert the dominant paradigm. No matter that this sentiment has more currency as a bumper sticker than as a core cultural value of the nineties. You can take the girl out of the counterculture, but you can't take the counterculture out of the girl.

Chelsea Cain
Portland, Oregon
August 1999

★ wild child

Zoë Eakle

Water Baby

zoë eakle

I guess my folks were trying out something new, but me, I never knew the difference. By the time I showed up they were already in British Columbia on the west coast of Canada. I was born in Sointula, the island of their destination.

Faded color photos create patchy images of who my parents were then. Snapshots of Dad with grown-out hair and thick dark beard, his jeans tucked into his gum boots, posing with home-grown hemp plants as tall as he is or sitting at the kitchen table pitting cherries from the tree in our backyard.

My mom's hair was long and straight and parted in the middle like a smooth dark stream around her freckled face. She said she didn't know what hard work was until they left the city. Pictures usually catch her in the middle of something, her sparkly eyes half closed from blinking at the camera. She is bending over a baby, or the dishes, or a row of weeding in the garden. Sometimes she is singing with a band on the front porch with a beer in her hand. Like my father, she is younger than I am today. Her long neck curves gently down into her back. She is beautiful.

And there's me, too young to remember myself, naked except for a hand-knit cardigan, crumbs or dirt on my face—it's hard to tell. I'm gazing earnestly into the camera. Staring up from a past turned to myth by memory and this word, "hippie," which apparently encompasses my childhood.

Sometimes when I introduce myself as Zoë, people ask, "Are your parents Greek?" And so I say, "No, they were hippies." I don't tell them the name presented itself to my parents during a particularly stellar acid trip. That would feed too much into expectation. Nevertheless, everyone gets an instant picture in their head. They are, of course, no closer to knowing the people in those snapshots.

When I go back to the island I try to imagine what my parents would have seen the day they moved there. What were their thoughts as they rumbled over potholes along the dusty gravel road? Blue-gray speckled rocks, driftwood and ocean on one side and on the other, merciless blackberry bushes guarding tall evergreens that stop just before the ceiling of the world. The forest interrupted here and there by clearings with small wooden homes.

It was late May, 1970. My parents had successfully crossed the border having declared their intention to emigrate, and had driven all day, anxious to reach the island. My mom was seven months pregnant with me, her first of two children. They were traveling in a GM panel truck, lovingly altered with a blowtorch to create Plexiglas skylights in the ceiling. They had asked a friend to install the windows right above where their heads rested on the sleeping platform. Underneath the platform lay all their worldly possessions.

The sun would be sinking low. Their truck would have just been transported from the ferry to the island by a Jaws of Life crane, with their dog barking on the passenger seat: The ferry didn't yet have a ramp that could support vehicles. They would be tired and eager to get to Sue's house, a drop-in mostly for American folks who had heard about Sointula and wanted to check it out. Did my father question the sanity of this venture? Did my mother wish for even a moment that she'd kept her job at the telephone company?

What the locals might have thought of all this activity is a book unto itself. Sointula was founded by Finnish immigrants in the late 1800s, who started a commune before communes were cool. They were sick of being used as cheap labor and decided to pool their resources and create a utopian community from the best of the communist and Marxist philosophies they had discussed back home. Sointula suffered many birthing pains but finally flourished in its small-town, island-unto-itself way. Although the utopian dream eventually fell by the wayside, it has never been entirely forgotten.

Then, along come these trippy hippie types to start a new way of living. The American hippies were mostly city folks and had no idea how to relate to the locals or even that they should. There were lots of Canadian alternative types all over doing the same thing and they undoubtedly had mixed reactions to these Americans coming in and taking over just by the sheer decibel of their enthusiasm.

Sue was Finnish, but had been raised in California. That afternoon when my parents turned into the gravel drive at her place, the first thing they saw was Sue's cedar-shake homestead to their right. Eight wide steps led up to its welcoming porch, big enough to comfortably seat the three or four folks who were probably there on that evening, smoking or drinking or toking or maybe all three. Maybe one or more people were tripping on mushrooms that night or groovin' on LSD, but probably not. Probably they were just hangin' out, listening to each other fill the night air with plans and stories. The Pacific Ocean drew itself to and from the shore across the street, murmuring watery sighs to itself under their rolling notes, paying them no mind.

It would have been just about twilight when they pulled into the drive. Twilight in Sointula will beckon your very soul. You can feel utterly alone there if you are in good company. That type of solitude is luscious. In those moments the land opens out to you and entreats you to breathe with it. Into the thousand different shapes of not-quite-round rocks on the beach, into the wild ocean and the barnacles and baby crabs. Breathe with the trees bowing and stretching into the wind. It is the kind of place that has convinced me in certain precious moments that I am no more or less marvelous than the rocks under my feet and the ocean before me.

There was also the little sauna to their left as they drove in, catching the last of the day's light on its two square windows. It had been converted for us into ten square feet of extra living space by a carpenter staying at Sue's. My parents had already decided that I would be birthed at home on the island. They had been researching the process for months. Sue was all for it too and had found lots of information. Even so, they probably didn't think as they drove up that day and passed by the little sauna, "That's where we'll have our first child and she'll be born with the sound of the ocean in her ears." Probably they gave Sue a hug and made a beeline for the outhouse around back. Dad had met Sue and her husband, Seth, at the University of California at Davis three years earlier. My parents spent a lot of time with them there, putting together seed orders and supplies to use in Sointula. They spent hours discussing political notions and the whole idea of having an open communal household, supporting draft dodgers and wanderers and the like. My parents were going to look after Seth and Sue's house and property for them while they spent a year in Hong Kong. Seth was working on his master's in Chinese philosophy.

The whole atmosphere around their place at that time felt radical and exciting. People were living out their ideals and dreams of a freer, more open life. A Vietnam medic who went AWOL after returning to the States came and stayed for a while. A black man who was all fun and play passed through. He was on the run from some Black Panther caper that we never really did find out about.

In the midst of all this, my parents moved into the sauna and made it their home. As summer wore on and Mom's due date got closer, a lot of people asked if they could help or just be there. In this manner the unofficial guest list grew, and grew.

My mom's parents were excited about the birth but knew nothing of the "home" part. My mom thought it best to spare them the anxiety and decided not to mention it. She suggested that they come a week or two after the due date. "By then," she said, "things will have calmed down a little and we can all have a nice visit."

I was due in June but like any well-grounded hippie child, I decided that I'd come on out whenever I was ready. Although I did not arrive in June, my grandparents did, along with my mother's sister from New York. My grandmother took one quick look around that room and knew. The eye drops and gauze, the *Whole Earth Catalog* earmarked in the birth section, the basic guide for mid-wives open on the kitchen table, the piles of fresh linen and buckets for extra water, all in a ten-by-ten space, were pretty much dead giveaways. My mom told my grandma that she'd understand if they wanted to leave and come back when the whole thing was over. My grandmother looked at her like now she truly had lost her mind and said they would be staying.

She took my grandfather for a walk and said, "They're going to have that baby at home you know." To which my grandfather replied, "No they're not," as though the simple force of his words could bring modern medical care to the island. He essentially remained in denial right up until my mother was fully dilated.

There were about fifty people there on the night I was born. There was plenty of home-brewed liquor on hand, undoubtedly there was music, a guitar or two and maybe even a banjo or a jew's-harp, and lots of potato salad. To this day everyone mentions the potato salad. Those homegrown potatoes are hard to beat.

My dad delivered me. My grandmother coached him. When Mom's afterbirth didn't come out right away, Dad was afraid to push her belly too hard and hurt her. My grandmother told him he bloody well better, and he did. All of us survived.

The AWOL medic was on hand that night, and he, along with several of my parents' friends, provided the invaluable service of ensuring that my grandfather got pie-eyed during the course of the affair. My grandfather was an operatic bass and I like to think he was singing drunken arias with the bluegrass band when I emerged.

Later, that sauna became a chicken shed; Sue and her partner built a new house higher up on the property; and the old homestead is used for storage now. It is so much smaller than I remember. Mold is beginning to creep up the walls but it still feels warm to me.

The sauna is gray and hollow, abandoned even by the chickens. I return the odd time just to stand there and look and try to see it as something other than Sue's chicken coop. The sun still filters in through those tiny windows and gaps in time in a way that whispers of a past I don't remember. Maybe one day somebody will decide that the whole area is an historical hippie site and they'll put a plaque on it: Sauna, Dwelling, Birthing Room, 20th Cent. (Actually, nailing a plaque onto that unassuming little structure would knock it down.)

Growing up in Sointula was in many ways grand. There were no locked doors and I had the whole forest, beach and ocean for a playground. There is a glimmer of peace inside me that comes from growing up in that place. My memory of Sointula goes beyond anything conscious to my salty core, which will always be grateful for having been born with the sound of the ocean in my ears. If nothing makes sense, I can look out over that vast body of water, and things won't necessarily make any more sense. But that's okay, because there I am with the whole Pacific Ocean at my feet.

Ariel Gore

Girl-child

ariel gore

Girl-child,

You asked me once if I was alive during the olden days.

I had to laugh. "What do you mean, the olden days?"

When I was a kid I'd pictured covered wagons and Model T Fords. You were thinking VW buses.

Later, at the winter assembly, your class sang "Free to Be You and Me," and you wondered how I knew the words.

Oh, I wish we still had a record player, girl-child, because I don't have Marlo Thomas on CD. Maybe if I could play it for you, then you'd understand something more than I can tell you about those olden days—before your grandmother's hair was gray (you know, she waited for you, didn't stop dyeing it until you were born), before I ever thought I'd be a mother myself (we worried about nuclear war then, not Y2K), before I was dragged in my torn bell-bottom cords to White Flower Day at Macy's (I would have saved those for you, girl-child, but who knew they'd be selling them at the mall now?), before kaleidoscope memory made your family history so hard to trace.

The stories circle now. They never quite line up. And you look at me cross-eyed as if to say, "Who are these freaks whose blood runs through our veins, Mama?" And what can I tell you?

These are the answers I was given as a kid:

My father was a merry prankster.

My sister was born in a tent during the summer of love.

My mother was sleeping with Henry Miller.

Or was it Ken Kesey?

No, Ken Kesey was a madman.

Ultimately, she seduced the local Catholic priest.

He wasn't supposed to marry her.

Vows, you know.

The family fortune is hidden behind door number two.

Millions.

No, billions.

My grandfather was a CIA plant.

Ours is not a family of pathological liars as you sometimes suspect, girl-child. But you have to understand something about the nature of memory, history, schizophrenia, and the long-term effects psychedelic drugs can have on the brain before you start taking anybody's word for anything.

What's that poem? That line? Childhood is a time when nobody dies? I don't know whose childhood they were talking about. When I was a kid they dropped like flies. The revolutionaries off their barstools. Mayors. City supervisors. Cult members and cult leaders. Bearded wanderers who called themselves "Wolf." The potters shot point-blank by their husbands—men who wouldn't see the insides of jail cells for two decades. Later, I'd stumble upon missives in the newspaper, "So-and-so finally brought to justice." The poets all climbed over the railing and flung themselves off the Golden Gate Bridge. I remember feeling sorry for one who survived. And relieved for her when I heard that she'd managed to drown herself in barbiturates and whiskey as soon as they had released her from the hospital. When I was a kid there seemed to me nothing quite so tragic as a failed suicide.

There were survivors, of course. There are always survivors. The poets moved into seclusion, up into the woods near Fort Bragg. The potters went back to school. Heald College. They learned computer programming basics and moved into condominiums. Invested quite wisely in the stock market.

The revolutionaries were diagnosed with manic depression. And the painters with paranoid schizophrenia.

At first your grandfather wouldn't take his medication. He said they were trying to kill him. But eventually he succumbed. Eventually, everyone succumbed.

And the children, we were scrubbed clean and dragged off to White Flower Day. Thrust suddenly and unprepared into innocence. Excessive sanitation. Hushed tones. A belated sober revelation that there are certain things children should not be told.

In that instant, as if by some mysterious curse, everyone stopped dying. Jeans were patched and pegged. Chocolate replaced carob. Margarine turned into butter. All the tastes changed. And all the smells. Pot and eucalyptus became roses and fresh paint. No one described hallucinations at the dinner table anymore. And I wondered: Did they stop seeing demons on their bedroom ceilings at night? Or did they just stop telling?

I was born on the Monterey Peninsula in the summer of 1970. Born to unmarried artists, refugees from Beverly Hills who had left everything but a flair for the dramatic and a nasty habit of name-dropping behind. Who had shrugged off the trust funds that weren't really there and left for the cooler waves that came crashing on northern sea cliffs and foggy shores. That much checks out.

You know, girl-child, there's something heart-breaking about your grandmother's poetry from those days. We—your aunt and I and the rest of the kids who used to huddle together on Saturday mornings before the grownups came to, huddle at the neighbor's house, in front of the forbidden TV, with spoonfuls of peanut butter and slabs of stolen ham—we were supposed to be the first generation of truly free children. Free to trample each other at the Bay School. Free to eat tofu and bean sprouts. Free of the sway of pop culture and advertising and Saturday morning cartoons. Free of finger bowls and social constructions of every kind. Free not to suffer from the eating disorders and gender-identity crises that weren't supposed to come later, but did. Of course they did.

Still, I was never nostalgic for the hopes in that poetry. I didn't miss the communal living and talk of nonviolent revolutions. I never did like the anarchist's free school.

When we moved to Palo Alto and Jimmy Carter morphed into Ronald Reagan and folk song circles became Amnesty International meetings, I didn't think of the olden days as tie-dyeing parties and Pacific Coast fields of Monarch butterflies. Yes, there had been that, too. But what I missed was the raw truth of it all. I missed the suicides and the open weeping. I missed believing that we would someday come into a family fortune. I missed my father, and all his colorful visions. I missed believing that someone was following us. That's what made us special, after all. We had the thickest FBI file. Didn't we? I'd always wonder.

When your grandmother finally settled down with my stepfather and they started shopping at Williams Sonoma, life got more predictable. More peaceful. But I missed the headlines and whispers behind our backs at the food co-op. He'd been a Catholic priest, after all. "Torn from the cloth by a temptress named Eve." I missed the journalists. I missed believing that our mother was the most scandalous woman on the block. I missed her altered states.

Their wedding song was Cat Stevens's "Morning Has Broken." But I missed the night.

I don't know if I spent my early years in the olden days, girl-child. An editor called this morning and asked me to describe a girlhood in the counterculture. I told her I wasn't sure I had one to tell.

Because, you know, the funny thing about olden days and modern days, about culture and counterculture, is the way they blend and blur. The way dawn can look just like dusk when you awaken disoriented after a day-long nap or a night-long sleep.

What culture are we living in now? Your grandmother curses my tattoos. Did she change? Or did I?

This morning you asked me to buy you peace-sign earrings at Clothestime, girl-child. Tonight the network newscasters told us straight-faced that the war was over. The smart bombs had done their job and all the casualties were friendly fire.

And sometimes I still wonder: Did everyone really stop dying? Or did everyone else just start lying?

Lisa Michaels

Our Mail Truck Days

lisa michaels

In 1969, my father was arrested for his part in an antiwar protest in Boston and was sentenced to a two-year prison term. (He and my mother had split up several years earlier, but they had remained close, sharing the child-rearing duties and trying to forge a new kind of divorce, one that was in keeping with their progressive politics.) He began serving his time at Billerica not long after his twenty-eighth birthday. I was a little over three years old. Once he was settled, my mother took me to see him in prison. He had written her a letter asking for books and a new pair of tennis shoes—he was playing a lot of pick-up basketball in the yard to keep his head clear. On the ride out to the prison, I clutched a box of black Converse hightops in my lap, my head bubbling with important things to tell him, thoughts which percolated up, burst, and disappeared—their one theme: Don't forget me.

I remember very little of our lives then, but that visit has the etched clarity and foggy blanks of a fever dream. We pulled into the broad prison parking lot and stepped out to face the gray facade punctured by a grid of tiny windows. Mother lifted her hand against the glare, then pointed to a figure in one of the barred openings. Was it my father? She hoisted me onto the roof of the car, and I held the shoebox over my head and shook it. I thought I saw the man wave back.

In the waiting room, the guards called our names in flat tones, never looking us in the eye. They led us through a series of thick pneumatic doors and down long corridors to the visiting room. Once we were inside, I saw something soften in their faces. "Sit right here, missy," one of them said. Mother lifted me into a plastic chair and my feet jutted straight out, so I stared at the toes of my tennis shoes, printed with directives in block letters: left, right.

I sat still until a door on the far wall opened and a flood of men filed in. Out of the mass of bulky shapes, my father stepped forward, the details of his face reassuring in their particulars. He grinned and reached for me across the tabletop scribbled with names and dates, and despite the no touching rule, the guards said nothing. When he took my hand, every manic bit of news I had practiced in the car flew out of me. I was stunned by the dry warmth of his skin, his white teeth, the way he cleared his throat in two beats before speaking. Distance made me notice for the first time these familiar things, which proved him to be real beneath the clipped hair and the prison uniform.

Our conversation was simple. There was little we could say in the span of one public hour. He read me stories, which my mother had brought, cracking the pages wide and roving from bass to falsetto as he acted out the dialogue. I told him what I ate for lunch, and in the silence before he answered I remembered the tennis shoes, flushed with relief to have something to give him. "Look what we got you," I said, and then tore the box open myself. I beamed and bunched my skirt between my knees while he admired them. "All Stars!" he said. "These are the best. I'm gonna tear up the court."

At the end of the hour, the guard rested one hand on his gun, tipped back on his heels, and called the time. Panic closed my throat. I looked to my father for a sign—he would tell the man we weren't ready—but his eyes were wet and the corners of his mouth twitched down. I turned to the stranger by the wall and flashed a saccharine smile. "Daddy," I asked, leaning my cheek on the table and looking at the guard, "is that the nice man you told me about?"

The guard squinched his face at me, in what passed for kindness in that place, then made a slow turn and gave us a few extra minutes. Once they were granted, we had nothing to say. I sat there with all my feeling funneled down to the smallest aperture, until my chest hummed and my head felt light. Then the guard said, "Time's up," and we shuffled to our feet.

In the clamor of chair legs and murmured good-byes, we could speak again. "Hey, what do you want for Christmas?" my father asked. I stopped in the doorway and stared at his dark bulk. I wanted him. But his voice was filled with a sudden expansiveness, and I knew I should ask for something he could give.

"Something purple," I told him. It was my favorite color then, and I let everyone know: I was staking out my turf in the visible spectrum.

I still have a letter he wrote me that night from his cell: "It may take a long time, but I'll try to get you a purple thing. Here's a pretend one for now." Below it is a necklace with a carefully sketched purple star, ringed by faint marks where I once tried to work it free from the paper.

This was the first of many letters he wrote me, each with a drawing in colored pencil. "Darling Lisa—Hello, Hello, Hello. I am very happy tonight. I got a guitar yesterday and am learning to play it. I am on a diet so I won't be fat at all—not even a little bit." Then half the page taken up by an abstract drawing: a grid filled with tangled clots of scribbling, a black anvil shape, a downward arrow, the symbol for infinity. "I call this picture, Being in Jail: JAIL. I love you darling, Your Father."

His notes were full of rhymes and playfulness: portraits of me with green hair, or of himself with the head of a man and the body of a conga drum. In places, his loneliness leaked through. "I will try to keep writing you," said one letter, "but it's hard when you don't write me back." I was pricked by guilt when I read these pleas, then quickly forgot them. At first his absence was a plangent note, always sounding in the background, but it became muffled as the months passed. In time, I had trouble recalling his face.

My mother made several visits to Billerica, but gradually she began to cut ties. My father had become increasingly focused on his political work in the months leading up to the demonstration, and his arrest meant she had no help in caring for me, no one to consult with, no air. She was furious at him, and fury made her feel free. We would move to Mexico and buy a piece of land. She would become a potter, maybe look for work teaching English. I would wear embroidered dresses and turn brown in the tropical sun.

In the flush of her new-found independence, Mother went to a postal service auction and bought herself a used mail truck. She parked it outside of our apartment and gave me a tour. With a tune-up and a few interior improvements, she said, it would get us south of the border. The cab had one high leather seat, and a long lever that worked the emergency brake. To shift gears, you punched numbered keys on a small raised box. It looked like a tiny cash register, and Mother let me play with it while the engine was off. A sliding door led back into a cold metal vault, bare but for a few mail shelves. "This is going to be our cozy rolling home," Mother said, her voice echoing off the walls.

For the next few months, my mother worked as a waitress and took steps to make the mail truck road-worthy. The first rains of autumn had revealed a couple of leaks in the chassis, so she spent a weekend driving around Cambridge in search of patching material. On a narrow side street, she spotted a promising sign: Earth Guild—We Have Everything.

She stopped in and asked the cashier if they had any sheet metal. The store was a kind of counterculture supermarket, stocked with incense, bolts of cotton, paraffin, books on homesteading, yarn and looms. But it seemed that "everything" didn't include sheet metal.

"What do you want it for?" the woman asked. It was a slow day in the store. Had there been a line of customers, impatient to buy beeswax and clay, our lives might have taken a different turn.

"I need to patch a hole in the side of my mail truck," my mother said.

"Well," the woman offered, "we don't have sheet metal, but we have Jim, and he has a mail truck, too." She yelled toward the back room, and out loped my future stepfather, a handsome lanky man in square-toed Frye boots, smiling an easy smile.

Jim came out to the curb and looked over the rust spots. He and Mother talked about their vans, how much they'd paid at auction, where they were headed. Jim also had his eyes on Mexico. And at the very moment my mother dropped by, he had been building a kiln in the back of the store for the Earth Guild's pottery studio. It seems she had stumbled on a man who could help her turn her schemes into brick and wood. By the time they finished talking, the sun was low in the sky and they had a date to change their oil together.

Jim had embraced the counterculture, but not on political terms. He wore hand-painted ties, listened to the Stones, and collected Op Art. When he met my mother, he was living in a commune in Harvard Square called The Grateful Union. "Those guys were uptown," my mother says. "Into spare living and Shaker furniture."

She and Jim soon made plans to head across the country under the same roof. We would take his truck, since it was considerably cozier than my mother's. A platform bed stretched across the width of the van, and a hinged half-moon table folded down from the wall and perched on one leg. We ate sitting cross-legged on the mattress. The walls were lined with bookcases, fitted with bungee cords to hold the volumes in place. On a shelf just behind the cab was our kitchen: a two-burner propane cooking stove, a tiny cutting board, and a ten-gallon water jug. Jim covered the metal floors with Persian rugs and hung a few ornaments on the wall: a plaque with the Chinese characters for peace, prosperity, and happiness; a yellow wicker sun.

Before we set out, Jim bought a small wood stove and bolted it to the floor near the back wall. The smokestack jutted out the side of the truck, the hole weather-sealed with the fringe from a tin pie plate. One of Jim's friends from The Grateful Union wired a stereo system into the van, and Mother sewed heavy denim curtains that attached to the window frames with velcro, so we could have privacy at night. The engine on these snub-nosed trucks bulged into the cab and was housed by a metal shell that served as a shelf for bags of mail. Jim cut a piece of thick foam just the shape of the engine cover, which would be my bed. A perfect fit. I was about the size, in those days, of a sack of mail.

In the spring of 1970, we packed up our essential belongings and set out on a year-long journey across the country, down the eastern seaboard and then across the low belly of the continent to California. The thrill of traveling sustained me for a while, but it was a difficult age to be rootless. I played with other kids for a day or two at a campground or a city park, and then we drove on. After a day on the road, Mother tucked me in on my foam pad, warmed from below by the engine's heat. In the footwell below me was a small pot we peed in during the night, and so I drifted off to the smell of urine and the tick of the cooling pistons. Now and then, when we were parked on some dark residential street, I would wake to the knock of a policeman, asking us to move along.

And move along we did, until our funds started to run thin, and Mother and Jim began to search for a piece of land, "our pie in the sky," as Jim called it. Mother was browsing through a copy of

Mother Earth News when she saw a classified ad listing land for sale. She located the town, which had a population of two thousand and was marked with the tiniest speck the map allowed, and we drove up through San Francisco headed for that dot.

We ended up buying a clapboard house in the heart of this coastal valley town, a half-acre plot that came with a stucco duplex. Later, Mother would say that you had to call the people who lived in those buildings homeless. Only two out of the four toilets worked. The ceiling plaster bloomed with stains. There were a handful of ramshackle sheds on the property and a line of rusted cars in the driveway. The yard was nothing but thistle and dry grass. They dickered with the landlord a little, and agreed to buy the place for $18,000.

Our new address was 10,000 Main Street. Apparently the town's founders had been anticipating an explosive growth period which never arrived. Just past our house, the only sidewalk in town ceased abruptly, the last slab jutting out toward the cow pastures and orchards down Powerhouse Road. We would hold down the end of the main drag, on about an acre of good river valley soil gone hard from neglect.

We moved into the front apartment, formerly inhabited by an old alcoholic woodcutter named Floyd, who died in his bed shortly after we arrived. It took us a week of scrubbing to make that place fit to live in. There was standing water in the sink that the neighbor told us hadn't been drained for six months. Mother made batik curtains for the windows, and lined the musty drawers with butcher paper. In the bedroom, the wallpaper hung in thick tatters, a yellowed flowery print laced with ribbons. We pulled that down and found a layer of cheese cloth tacked beneath it, and when that was stripped away, solid foot-wide redwood planks, rough planed from trees that must have been five hundred years old.

I was given Floyd's bedroom. Mother and Jim slept in the living room on a bed that doubled as a couch by day. I was not yet five, and it was summer, so I had to go to bed before the sun went down, which felt like exile from the world of light. I would press my face against the screen and watch the older neighborhood kids playing kickball in the street or straddling their bikes on the corner. One evening, not long after we had moved into the house, my mother and Jim came to tuck me in, and the two of them lingered for a moment. Mother sat on the edge of my bed and sang to me. Jim stood in the middle of the room with his hands in his pockets, looking out the western window at the torn-up yard, the bristle of cattails in the ditch, and the corrugated roof of Mel's welding garage across the street, where he went every afternoon to buy glass bottles of Coke from the vending machine.

The novelty of the two of them tucking me in together in my very own bedroom set me humming with pleasure, and I wanted to say something in honor of this, but I didn't dare break their reverie. Even as I lay there, mute with happiness, I was conscious of the fragility of the scene—two parents, one child, pausing for a few moments together under one roof at the day's end.

Late in the summer of 1971, when I was nearly five, my father was released from prison. Friends of his were living on a commune in Oregon, and they had invited him to come and sort himself out.

He came west, as soon as he was free, and gathered me from Mother's place.

It must have been a shock to see him again, for I have no memory of our first hours together. I know we took a Greyhound bus up to Eugene, and a friend from the commune picked us up and drove us out to the property—acres of dry grass and scrub oak. There, my memories become clearer. The commune members were roughing it—no running water, no electricity, just a few ramshackle houses at the end of a long dirt road.

My father's attempt to unwind in the woods was a disaster. The sudden move from a cell to the wilderness seemed to leave him nervous and unsettled. The first day he tried to play the hip nudist and got a terrible sunburn. Then he drank some "fresh" spring water and spent three days heaving in the outhouse. I stayed indoors with him while he recovered, making him tell me stories. "Me and nature never got along," he said.

But as the days drifted on, we settled into the place. My father taught me to use a BB gun in the field beside the commune's main house. Arms around me from behind, he cheered when we shot the faded beer cans off the stump. "Sock it to me," he would say, holding out his enormous, olive-colored palm. We ate homemade bread and black beans which the women in the main house prepared, swam naked in the creek flowing through the property. One wall of the room we shared was given to me as painting space. I spent the afternoons scribbling figures on the white paint as high as I could reach, faces with huge, lidded eyes and no mouths, rapt but mute.

One day we wandered into one of the many rough-framed

buildings on the property to take shelter from the midday heat. Cinder block and knotty pine bookshelves lined the walls. Up near the ceiling, a long sagging board supported Lenin's collected works. A sink and countertop unit pulled out of a remodeled kitchen shored up one wall. There was no running water; spider webs stretched from the tap to the drain. A propane stove sat on the drainboard, and beneath it, on the floor, were jugs of cooking fuel and water.

My father moved to the open door, raised his arms up to the door frame and stretched like a cat. He was there in body—a body honed by hours in the weight room, on the courts playing ball with the other prisoners—but in another way he was fitfully absent. At five, I was having trouble pinpointing this. He circled the room slowly, traced a pattern in the countertop's dust, not pent up, but aimless, as if he had lost something and didn't know where to search. I squatted near the sink, playing with a set of plastic measuring cups, watched him closely. He moved through the doorway—for a moment framed by light, a dark cutout of a man—then passed out of view.

Thirsty, I decided to make a tea party. I went outside to see if my father wanted to play, and found him sprawled under a large oak tree near the door. He was staring up at the leaves, his hand spread open in the air above him, and didn't answer at first.

"Do you want some tea?"

He raised his head and his eyes slowly focused, placing me. "No thanks, honey."

I went back into the shack and filled two of the cups from a jug on the floor. I pretended to have a partner for my tea, and chatted with him a while before drinking from my cup, thumb and forefinger on the short handle, my pinkie raised high.

From the first sip I could tell something was wrong. The water burned my tongue, and when I opened my mouth to scream all the air in the room was gone, there was only fierce vapor. I spat out what I could and yelled, feeling a white heat unfurl down my throat. My father dashed in, smelled my breath and the spilled gas and scooped me up from the floor. He ran with me toward the spring and over his shoulder I watched the shack jiggling smaller and smaller in the field. It seemed lonely, canted off to one side on its foundation like a child's drawing of a house. The dry, summer hay swayed like the sea, and I heard his breathing, ragged as surf.

When we reached the spring, a bearded man was there filling a green wine bottle. Water spilled down a rock face into a pool bounded by ferns and moss. My father gasped out the story and together they hovered over me, making me drink from the bottle again and again. "That's good," they said. "You're doing really good." My father stroked my hair. And though I wanted to stop, I tipped my head back and drank for him.

That night we stayed in the main house. My lips and throat were chapped and burning. I began to have visions. A crowd of ghosts led by a goateed figure marched with torches through the room. I told this to the grownups and they seemed alarmed. Some of the other people staying at the house lit extra kerosene lanterns to soothe me, but I could still see the figures. The leader looked furious, driven, his whole body straining forward toward some unknown mission.

My father moved with me to a bedroom upstairs and held

me in a worn corduroy arm chair, talking softly, telling me stories of what we would do together when it was light. The vagueness I felt in him during the day had disappeared. He was dense, focused, his legs pressed long against the sides of the chair, his arms around me heavy and still. I sat in his lap, leaning into the rise and fall of his chest. In my last rinse of delirium, I closed my eyes and saw his body supporting me like a chair, the long, still bones, and under him the real chair, fabric stretched over wood, and all of this twenty feet above the ground on the upper floor of the house, held up by the beams and foundation, and beyond that the quiet fields, silver under the moon, alive with animals, the punctured cans lying still by the stump. I saw us perched in the center of this, neither safe nor doomed, and in this unbounded space I fell asleep.

Angela Lam

Strange and Wonderful

angela lam

Sometimes in your life someone gives you permission to be exactly who you are. For me, that person was Nina.

Let me explain: I grew up listening to the Eagles, Air Supply and ABBA and watching *The Monkees* and *The Brady Bunch* on TV. I gave my Barbies first and last names and family histories. I learned to count to one hundred before kindergarten and tie my shoes before anyone else in class. I was the only one I knew of with more than one sibling and more than one parent living at home. I had a mixed heritage, half Chinese, half German; I conversed in English and cursed in Cantonese at school and at home. I attended Mass every Sunday and learned to pray the rosary. On birthdays and special occasions, I traveled with my family to San Francisco where we sat in banquet halls with hundreds of five-foot Chinese relatives, aunts and uncles and cousins twice removed who spoke Cantonese, ate fifteen-course meals and toasted with sparkling cider to happiness and good luck.

Outside of my family, my father said, there was no one you could trust. The world was a dangerous place, my father said. The only safe place was home. Now, nearly twenty years later, I know that sometimes it is dangerous to be safe. Sheltered—that's how my friends and colleagues put it. My childhood, that is. Fiercely protected by a father I respected and feared as much as I loved, I grew up in the shadow of rules and regulations, of "Don't do this" and "Don't do that." When other children were going to birthday sleepovers, I stayed home. It was dangerous at other people's houses, my father reasoned. You never knew what was going on, what hurtful games children played, what danger parents either ignored or allowed.

Afraid of my being molested, my father taught me about sex when I was old enough to understand the word "no." By the time I was seven, I knew I was conceived by a bodily function, not delivered by a stork. There were other disclosures, too. When other kids believed in the tooth fairy and Santa Claus, I knew neither existed. My father tried to rob me of an imagination. Instead, he created a girl who would conjure up worrisome events that never happened, who would dream of disaster before it occurred, who would lie awake at night with a tummy ache and a headache and her mind in a whirl. Nothing was safe, although much was sacred. The body, especially. And the mind.

I remember wondering what a normal childhood was all about. I remember trying desperately to make friends. I remember being told to keep secrets, to protect my honor. Even with a lie— although I didn't lie, not early on. I remember these things the way some people remember a drunken relative or an abusive parent. With fear, with avoidance. But running only makes the past easier to find you. It is better to stay still and let history wash over you and cleanse the pain.

"Everything is dangerous," my father told me. "Trust no one."

The year Summer and her family moved in was the worst. I broke promises. I told lies. I kept secrets. I woke with tummy aches and headaches from fear of discovery. Sometimes it is easier to be caught and to deal with consequences than to escape. For the prison of your mind holds no escape, and your heart does not forget.

Everything is dangerous, my father said. Trust no one.

How then shall I trust you?

It was July 1979, the year before Reagan and voodoo economics, the year before my cousin Ken bought his first suburban house, the year my mother returned to work full-time, the year I started babysitting my two younger sisters and taking on more and more responsibility around the home.

Summer and her family, a group of vagabond hippies, moved into the house at the end of the block. "Renters," my father told me. "Just as bad as criminals," he said. Of course, they were not to be trusted.

Curious as any eight-year-old, I spied on the new neighbors. I crept up to the front window and peered into the living room. Nothing telling of what evils awaited me there. The room was empty except for a tattered brown recliner and a standing lamp. Not even a TV. The house seemed lonely, sad. A little lost. I didn't think about it anymore until school started and the bus picked up one of the new neighbors, a tall, thin girl with stringy golden-brown hair and dreamy eyes. She wore floral and tie-dyed dresses and open-toed sandals even in the rain. She smiled and laughed a lot at things other kids did not find funny. She did not curl her hair or wear jeans when everyone else thought it was cool. When kids called her names, she made a sign with her hands. "Peace and love," she'd say.

I was enchanted.

She was a year older than I was and every bit as mysterious as her name. Summer. A promise of warm weather and clear skies and swim parties and suntans and lazy afternoons at the beach. When she waltzed by the playground, her long hair drifted like seaweed. On the jungle gym bars, she was the only girl unafraid of swinging upside down with a skirt on and letting the boys see her cotton underwear. There was a lack of inhibition about her, an I-couldn't-care-less about the judgment of others, a spring in her step. Everything about her, from her unkempt hair to the silver beads on her wrists, spoke of magic. When she confided in me that she knew witchcraft, I believed her.

I grew to trust her like I trusted my sisters, implicitly, without words.

One day, Summer invited me over to her house after school. "I can show you my record collection," she said. When she smiled, I knew I would say yes, even though I knew the answer from my father would be no.

But I was still my father's daughter, honest and obedient, eager to please. I asked him when he got home from work. He took me aside and closed the door to his bedroom and said, "I don't want you playing with that girl. She looks like a tramp. I bet her parents make her walk the streets at night. She's not a good influence for you or your sisters. I do not want you going to her house."

My mother offered a compromise. "Invite her over here to play."

But I wanted to see her record collection. The color of her room. The width of her bed. The closet that stored her clothes.

A week later, when Summer asked again if I could come over, I said yes. I did not tell her my parents forbade it. It was my first lie, my first secret, and the power of it burned in my stomach like a hot fist.

I jumped off the bus and headed across the street and into the empty living room of Summer's home. A warm sweet scent arrested me. Summer grabbed my hand and led me down the hall through a beaded rainbow-colored curtain and into her room. I sat down in a beanbag beside the unmade twin bed with its rumpled sheets and strong odor of dogs and urine and something else, something I did not recognize. Summer opened her closet door and withdrew albums I had never heard of. She gathered the ones she liked best and we stepped into the family room where a teenage boy lounged on a sofa with his arms around two teenage girls. "That's my brother, Sky," she said. "And his girls, Tina and Lori." Another young man with long hair and a beard sat cross-legged on the shag carpet strumming a guitar. "That's Hunter," she said. "My mother's brother." An older woman with a long braid down her back rocked in a hammock. "That's Nina, my father's mother."

Without asking permission, Summer proceeded to play Jimi

Hendrix's "Manic Depression," "Break on Through to the Other Side," by the Doors, and Pink Floyd's "Comfortably Numb." Hunter stood up and retreated to the kitchen and returned with a bowl of steamed vegetables and a glass of water, which he passed around the room. Tina stood up and adjusted her bikini top and said she was going to make an alfalfa sandwich and pour herself a glass of goat's milk. Sky paused from kissing Lori and patted Tina's bottom and said, "Go get us something, too."

Tina glanced down at me. "Would you like something to eat?"

I remembered my father telling me never to eat or drink anything at anyone's home: The food could be poisoned; the drinks could contain alcohol; I could get sick, maybe die. "No, thank you," I said.

From across the room, Nina beckoned me. I expected to be reprimanded. But she gathered me into the hammock and wrapped her arms around my chest and said, "I want to tell you a story. About how we came here." Her deeply bronzed skin creased when she smiled. "We started in New York—Brooklyn, to be exact. Nothing to talk about there. Just smutty skies and mean-spirited people. Summer's father met Yellow Bird at a concert in Central Park, and they decided to run away together. That was the year Summer was born. I went with them. There was nothing in New York for me. Nothing worth mentioning, that is. We packed our belongings into two duffel bags. We had a roll of quarters and hearts full of love and hope. After spending the night on a park bench, we found a trucker going west. Said he'd drop us off in Chicago. We didn't like it there, too much like New York, and we wanted to see the Grand Canyon, so we found another trucker going west and headed out again. Never did make it to the canyon. Got stuck somewhere in Idaho. Walked twenty miles in the snow. Don't ask me how. We were young and invincible." Nina hugged me tight against her chest. "Tell me, child, do you believe in magic?"

I thought of the life-size statue of Jesus nailed to the cross, and the promise of eternal life. I guessed it must be magic. "Of course," I said. "When we die, we live forever."

Nina nodded and looked entranced by the thought of eternity. "We come back sometimes, you know. Depending on how good we are and what we've done. I was an eagle once. I flew so high I could kiss the clouds. I bet you were a coyote or a wolf. You have the hunter in you, child. A brave soul. Of fire and water. A daughter of the moon." She touched my eyelids with her fingertips. "Even your eyes are like crescent moons."

I thought of my father saying I was nothing because I was a girl. In China, girls are bad luck. A curse on the family. I knew I was lucky. I had been born in America to an American woman and allowed to live, not forgotten and drowned in a well.

But I liked Nina's story better, of how I was the daughter of the moon, a brave soul, a hunter.

Nina twirled a brown beaded necklace around her neck. The beads clacked in time with the rhythm of the music. Nina's skin creased into folds above her eyebrows and beside her mouth. There was a peacefulness about her, a quiet consistency that echoed in the room. I wanted to know her better, to feel her leathery skin against my palm, to listen to more of her stories.

A sliding glass door opened, and a naked woman entered from the backyard. Nina introduced her as Sally. She was Summer's mother's sister. An aunt. Only no one called her that. They called her Sally. I remember turning away from her nakedness, a sight I did not want to acknowledge, although everyone else looked and did not say a word. In my home, the body was hidden and ignored or protected from strangers. Sally rubbed her arms and her breasts and her belly and her thighs with a large terry cloth towel and massaged lotion into her skin.

"Sunbathing," Nina explained. To get the bronze Nina had. I wondered about my yellow skin, how it would deepen in the sun, and I thought about how much trouble I would be in if I ever stripped down to nothing and lay outside to burn.

Sally slipped into a bikini and joined us. Hunter grabbed a bowl with a pipe and announced it was time for a peyote feast. Sky and his girls gathered around on the carpet. Nina and Summer joined them. I stood, waiting to be invited. Nina smiled and patted the space beside her. I slipped between Nina and Summer and felt exhilarated and frightened. My chest tightened in the billows of sweet-smelling smoke. The bowl and pipe were passed around the circle after each person inhaled a few breaths. When it was my turn, the heat from the pipe stung my throat. I coughed and choked. My head spun. Nina's face, with its gentle brown creases, grew large and floated like a giant moon in a pale sky. She shook my shoulders gently. "Are you all right, child? Breathe. Deeply. From the bottom of your chest. Feel your belly expand. That's right. Slower. Steady, now. Don't go too fast. That's it. Do you want to try again?"

I did not know whether or not I wanted to try again. Someone was knocking on the front door. Someone was yelling my name. My mother.

Hunter answered the door. Nina joined him. Voices rose and fell. I thought about the hurt in my belly, the tightness in my chest, the swelling in my head. I did not want to go home to precision and order, responsibility and consequence, rules and regulations, silence and lack of love. I wanted to stay in the chaos of smoke and music and exotic foods and vivid stories, of nakedness and openness and acceptance and love. I wanted to sleep beside Summer with her arms around me, her naked belly pressed against my naked back, not alone with an armor of cotton around me. I wanted to listen to the strange rhythms of guitars, not to the sappy love songs or brokenhearted tunes my mother played on the radio. More than anything, I wanted the freedom of Summer's world.

Nina drifted around the corner, looking for me. "Your mother is asking about you," she said. "I told her not to worry. I would walk you home."

I stood up, dizzy and nauseated. Nina linked her arm around my waist and led me outside. I could see my parents' house down the street with its yellow stucco and bright red trim. My family was different. I knew how others judged us—except for Summer and her family. They were different, too.

I stared at Nina's bare feet against the pavement. She smiled and wiggled her toes. "I can feel the vibrations of the earth on its axis. It is the pulse of the universe."

"Aren't you afraid of stepping on glass and cutting your feet?"

"All cuts heal." Nina hugged me close. Her flowing gown smelled damp. "Nothing can be broken that can't be fixed, you understand? We are human, strange and wonderful. We are meant to be broken. By pain. By grief. By disappointment. By each other.

But we are made whole through love and forgiveness. Remember that, and you will never be lonely."

She stroked my hair and kissed my cheek. "I hope you come visit us again." Though I did not say it, I knew I would never again be allowed back into Summer's home. Nina and I walked, hand in hand, down the sidewalk and across the street. Nina stopped at the front door and waited until my mother answered. No words were exchanged. My mother's angry stare bored into me. I shuddered in my skin, already feeling her icy words in my body, her violent pleas to be obedient, to honor my father's demands.

After I stepped inside, I bolted for my room and closed the door. My mother did not knock, but just stepped inside and said, "Tell me what possessed you to go over to that girl's house when your father told you not to? I was worried sick, don't you understand? I knocked on every neighbor's door. No one knew where you were. I called the police. I called your father at work. I thought you had been kidnapped and raped and killed. I thought you were never coming home."

Tears crested in my half-moon eyes. I held my breath, determined not to let them fall.

"You know better than to sneak around behind our backs. You are grounded for a month. I'm going to have your grandfather pick you up at school and bring you home. I'm going to call from work and make sure you answer the phone. You're a disgrace to our family and a poor example to your sisters. Just wait until your father gets home."

My mother stormed out of the room and banged pots and pans in the kitchen as she attempted to cook dinner. My head ached.

My stomach churned. I felt so bad I wanted to die.

At dinner, no one spoke of my transgressions, though my sisters glanced at me with furtive eyes. My father was not home. He did not return from work until late at night when we were supposed to be asleep.

The following morning, my father called me into his room. "You embarrassed us," he said. "What will people think of us if they saw you at that slum? What type of parents will they think we are for letting you go over there?"

I did not know and I did not care, but I was told I should know, I should care. So I did.

I listened to my parents. I let my grandfather pick me up after school when everyone else rode the bus. I let my mother call me from work to see that I was home, caring for my sisters like I said I would. I let my father lecture to me about good people, honest people, trustworthy people.

A week before Christmas, Summer and her family moved as mysteriously as they had appeared. By January, another family had moved in, a more conventional one, with a mother and a father and two children, a boy and a girl, both of whom did not want to play with me or my sisters, even after my father said it was okay. "They go to our church, be nice to them," my father reasoned. But they kept to themselves as much as we did.

Only once did my father speak of Summer's departure, and when he did, he dramatized it as if it were a made-for-TV movie. "They left in the middle of the night. They had something to hide and did not want to get caught. They didn't have a moving van. Just a truck. They piled up furniture and left the place a mess. The owners had to paint and re-carpet and replace doors and the stove. They left trash everywhere. And they never paid rent. Not once."

I missed Summer. I missed the escape into a world where time did not matter, where tasks could be forgotten, where it was just fine to be. I wanted stories like Nina's to tell my children someday.

Years passed. I forgot about Nina and Summer—for a time. When I was nineteen, I moved 110 miles from home and lived with my boyfriend. A year later, I married. Three years later, I had a son. For five years, I did not own a TV. I listened to whatever my husband played on the stereo. I walked barefoot and naked in the house. I have stories to tell. Of my wedding reception: how the best man had broken his toe and was downing vodka to numb the pain and when the time came for his elegant speech, he wavered with his glass and said, "Get a life!" We laughed. Guests and relatives cowered with shame. It is a tale I tell strangers when they want to get to know me.

I still have problems trusting others and myself. I keep secrets. I exaggerate. Sometimes I lie. When others berate me and demand perfection, I forget to open my heart and offer them forgiveness and love. Many nights, even with my family home, I feel alone.

I'm still looking for that freedom. Sometimes I see it when I grow out my hair, wear clothes that are no longer in style, disregard consequences. I see Summer in the man I married, a man who is proud of his body, relishes his talents, doesn't weigh the opinions of others more than his own, a man who has seen my body change from a back injury, a pregnancy, an abortion, and who loves me more each day for the woman I was, the woman I am, the woman I will someday become. I hear Nina's voice in the stories I tell: delivering an unapproved valedictory speech at my high school graduation, leaving my boyfriend to date his best friend, having sex at a construction site high above the city lights, writing love letters to a writer whose work I fell in love with long before I fell in love with him, taking my three-month-old son with me to work, nursing him during my ten-minute breaks, nourishing him with my milk, my presence, my poetry, my love.

Each day is full of discovery. I give myself permission to be whoever I am, a spirit of fire and water, a daughter of the moon, a brave soul, a hunter, a wife, a mother, a writer, a woman.

Elizabeth Shé

Free Love Ain't

elizabeth shé

We wore robes everywhere, and flowers in our hair. We made sand castles on Venice Beach. We painted our house bright orange and yellow and red and named it Rainbow Flower. Our bathroom featured a mural of giant mushrooms and fairies with glow-in-the-dark stars and a crescent moon. We skinny-dipped on Oregon beaches. We drank alcohol, smoked pot. My brother surfed before he could walk. And Jimi Hendrix played with agonizing consistency in our house, driving me to a seven-year-old's distraction. I still can't listen to "Foxy Lady" without cringing. And the smell of marijuana makes me ill.

My mother was raised Catholic. When my parents divorced (I was six), she ran hell-bent for leather in the opposite direction. Suddenly realizing that being a good girl nets you nothing, she tried the other extreme: sex, drugs and rock 'n' roll. My good little Catholic mom drank and fucked like a sailor. For her birthday, we made her a macramé bell system over her bed that she rang with her toe when she orgasmed.

Sexual innuendos came fast and furious in our house. The randier a joke, the funnier it was. No matter that neither my baby brother (six years younger) nor I knew what the hell we were laughing at. For my tenth birthday, my mom organized a striptease for me and my friends, with bawdy music from *The Sting* and racy nightgowns. I learned to masturbate with my Chatty Cathy.

Sex is fun. Sex is a game. Sex is sport.

The free love movement was a wonderful theory. My parents and their friends were reacting to war, to violence, to governmental betrayal. They wanted a better world, and thought free love was a way to achieve it. Make Love Not War. All You Need Is Love.

Merriam Webster's Collegiate Dictionary defines free love as "sexual relations without any commitments by either partner." But let's break it down.

Free. Definition number fifteen states: "open to all comers." Oh, yeah, baby. That was definitely how my parents' circle of friends was operating in the sixties and seventies. The good dictionary goes on to say, "*Free* stresses the complete absence of external rule"— yep—"and the full right to make all of one's own decisions." Kids too?

Love. Definition number seven: "copulation." That's it—no need to read further.

Free love meant sex, and lots of it. Free love meant you did it anywhere and everywhere to prove you were hip, unencumbered by society's rules. Countering her strict religious upbringing, my mother was born again, as a twentieth-century fox. She slept with a fifteen-year-old, a twenty-year-old, a musician or three, a forty-year-old accountant. I heard her sexual ecstasies from my bedroom. The bells over her bed rang frequently.

I was a wild child of a newly minted wild child.

Hippies were outside of society, better than society. I still remember a family friend saying I was too good to like a certain black-humored movie. My mother chirped right up. "She's not good. She's bad." Good is bad and bad is good. No wonder I'm in therapy.

I have an immediate negative response to people who smoke pot and wear bell-bottoms. Unfortunately for me, my college campus is full of people who nostalgically look at the sixties as the pinnacle of our century. But they weren't there. They weren't even born. They didn't see the day after the wild orgy, when my four-year-old brother wandered into the kitchen for a snack, and had to dodge the flying wine bottle my mother was throwing at her drummer boyfriend. Yeah, we were free. Free to fuck our siblings, or drink screwdrivers until we puked.

But not free to say no.

The free love movement, in practice, set me up for a lifetime of sexual, emotional and physical abuse. I learned that sex is a should. If someone wanted to sleep with me, I let him. It didn't matter—never mattered—if I didn't want to. Free only went one way. And love meant sex.

If you ask me, free love ain't either. It's not love, and it's not free. I've been paying the price for thirty years.

When I was in the third grade, my babysitter ran away from home to live with us, staying more than a year. Several teenage boys started hanging around, and some girls, adding to the hormonal stew. We called them The Teenagers. Suddenly I had older siblings, and I loved it. I was free to act like a kid, not the responsible elder taking care of my mother. And my mom got to be even more of a wild child—experimental, free and easy. No worries.

One day my babysitter's friend Geoff said we should bond. He sliced my hand, then his, and smeared our blood together. I was nine. He was on acid. My new blood brother leered at me when his girlfriend left the room.

My mother's brother also leered at me, as did a few of my father's friends. There was nowhere, after I developed breasts, that I was safe.

My dad felt free to comment on strangers' bodies—even those of twelve-year-olds. And I wonder why I've always hated mine?

What I learned as a child of the sixties—fuck everything that moves and let it fuck you—has definitely shaped my adulthood. Want to screw on the beach? Want to fuck under the desk at work? in the alley? on the side of the road? in the car driving eighty miles an hour?

Sure.

My function on earth, said society, said the hippies, said my mother, was to be fuckable. Extremely fuckable. Did I want sex? Who cares? Open your legs and let me in or I'll call you a square, mainstream, conservative. God forbid.

My brother and I saw our mother say yes to everyone, so we learned to say yes to everyone, even strangers. When I was fourteen, I was molested by a talent agent. When my brother was twelve, he was molested by his best friend's father.

Sex. Not simple, not easy, not free. And not love.

My mom routinely took us to the Fox Theatre to watch movies. We popped our own popcorn and smuggled in thermoses of Gallo wine (unless we were boycotting). Once she dragged us to *Performance* and something I only remember as *Bye-Bye Blackbird*. Both rated R, both semi-pornographic. Nuns sodomized and killed. Mick Jagger fucking a starlet.

My brother cried for a month with nightmares, and twenty years later, I still vividly remember those violent images. Some things are too graphic for kids to see, but we saw them, and later tried them, or at least consented to them.

It may be why, years later, I beg a boyfriend to whip me. And, more recently, why I throw up when a new friend wants to shop in a sex store.

No boundaries, no guidance, no protection. Nothing was sacred.

And yet, as a kid, everyone envied me my mother. She let me do anything I wanted. I could roam the streets after midnight on a school night, or fuck a classmate on an open field after a football game. All she wanted was the details, which she promptly passed on to her friends, along with the size of my brother's dick.

My hippie mother even suggested people for me to sleep with, didn't understand when I wouldn't, especially if it was someone she wanted. She saw nothing wrong with the local mechanic taking pictures of me naked. After all, he took some of her.

Neither parent provided protection. I think my mom naively believed that all you do need is love, that love will heal all wounds, that there is no such thing as inherent evil. She couldn't imagine such evil, so couldn't guard against it. After a while, in self-defense, I lied to my friends about curfews (that I had one) and restrictions (that I had some). I wanted limits before I got eaten up. But by then it was too late.

I slept with my best male friend (to Pink Floyd, of course). I slept with my best friend's boyfriend. All this would've been fine and dandy except I felt like shit. One of my friends laughingly called me a slut, but I knew she meant it. Another girlfriend wrote me a nasty letter after I slept with a guy I hadn't known she liked.

As I got older, I did my best to have a protective boyfriend around, someone to fall back on, so I had a "legitimate" excuse to turn people down. As if what I wanted didn't count. Sorry, can't ménage à trois. My boyfriend, you know.

The fifteen-year-old my mother bedded became my lover fifteen years later. My mother abused him, he later abused me. Instigated by good ol' free love.

I guess I'm lucky to be alive. I have no STDs, I'm HIV-negative. But free love exacted a terrible price on my family. These days I trust no one either over or under thirty. I have no real friends, no support, no closeness. Neither my brother nor I can keep a meaningful relationship going for very long before it self-destructs. We've both been in jail for domestic violence, and we both continue to flail in the maze of our desecrated sexuality.

Free love freely fostered self-hatred, which manifested itself in eating disorders and suicidal tendencies. I became so disconnected from my body that my gynecologist would find objects (tampons, condoms) left in my vagina for days. I didn't feel them rotting inside me.

I was primed to be the sexiest, the wildest, the least hung up. Liberal. A hippie's kid. Untainted by rules and regulations. Unconstrained. Free.

These days I have so many hang-ups, I'm surprised I can walk down the street without tripping. And actually, there were years when I *couldn't* walk down the street; I couldn't even leave my house. Nowhere was safe except, paradoxically, my bed. Depression and sex, with bed as part of the disease and the cure.

If you saw me now you'd have no inkling that I used to dance to the blues in such a way that the musicians all had hard-ons, that my favorite movie, after *The Rocky Horror Picture Show*, was *9 1/2 Weeks*.

Today I rarely wear revealing clothes outside of the house. I don't like dirty jokes or double entendres, and I hate Valentine's Day, with its corresponding message, "Everybody copulate!" Some would call me frigid.

Elizabeth Shé ✪ 59

I read self-help books that say sex is healthy, sexual urges are normal, I'm not a slut. But that vaguely echoes what my mother taught me. Sex is good. Sex is fun. Sex is sport.

Nowadays I have only fantasies, because I am too damn tired to deal with people. After so many years of sexual abuse, and being the sexiest slut on the block, ironically, I can't have sex.

For a period of time, I cried every time I came, and exhibited signs of post-traumatic stress disorder. I gained weight, wore baggy clothes, shaved my head.

I call myself bisexual, but in truth, I'm asexual. Celibate. Scared even to flirt. Because flirting leads to sex—inevitably, mandatorily, to sex. So I don't even start. Everyone I know is safely partnered up.

Deep down inside I am conservative. I don't like multiple lovers, I only want to sleep with one person. I pretended to separate sex from love, but I was only fooling (and abusing) myself. Sex *was* love for me—a substitute love—not sport, not just fun. Love my body, love me. Simple, easy. Not.

I have a hard time imagining someone really loving me unless I fuck her into the ground. As if sexual prowess ensures love or even monogamy. The well-trained concubine.

Now I am scared of anything sexual, afraid I can't control myself, that I'll eke back into my yay-saying ways. I'm afraid to do anything other than write and fantasize.

But I'm lonely. Lonely for love, for companionship, for touch. My body betrays me by craving caresses, coveting kisses, melting under hugs. I am a sensual being. All the ugly, baggy clothes in the world won't stop my body from responding to smells, sounds, touches, tastes. My sex drive rears its ugly head frequently. Repression only works for so long. Eruption is imminent.

Eventually I'll have to reconcile this with the sex abuse. Every month (probably hormonal) I get horny, masturbate, then feel extraordinarily degraded and ashamed. Bad.

Not good.

I've taken to writing violent pornography which offends my feminist sensibilities, but for some reason *(Bye-Bye Blackbird?)* keeps coming up. I read porn too, and it shames me.

Ten thousand dollars in therapy bills later, the love I gained through sex, or free love, is nonexistent.

The cost of "free" love? Self-esteem. Happiness.

A few things have changed. The Beatles are still gods, but my mother has had plastic surgery. And I am slowly healing from my parents' fling with free love. I guess the pendulum had to swing to the other extreme for me to achieve balance. I'm learning that not everything is black or white. I can grab the grays and define them. I just hope I recognize the happy medium when it hits.

When I come out of my promiscuity backlash, my own little frigid movement, I hope to feel safe and powerful *and* sexual. Something I can almost imagine. But not quite.

I *am* learning that I am free to choose. I can choose whom to kiss, whom to embrace, whom to love. Just because someone likes the looks of me doesn't mean I have to jump in the sack. *I* can decide how it's going to go. And it's not an all or nothing proposition. I can explore a few feet down that path, then stop and turn around.

My parents, happy practitioners of free love, didn't teach me safety, or boundaries. But I am teaching myself these things. Out of love—the real stuff.

Carin Clevidence

Seeing Belize

carin clevidence

When they fished the dead man out of the Rio Hondo we were surprised that he was yellow. One of the fishermen from the village saw him floating in the river; by the time they brought him to shore, at the far end of San Antonio where the houses gave way to jungle, most of the village had turned out to look. My mother, the only one with a camera, was asked to photograph the body. My little sister Shelly and I tagged along, but at the edge of the field we hung back, peering out from behind a banana tree. The man was naked. He'd died from machete wounds to the groin, a fact we learned much later. The men from the village carried the body past us on a sheet of canvas. He had been in the river long enough for the water to bleach him yellow. "Look at his ears," Shelly whispered. His ears were nearly gone, chewed away like his nose and his fingertips by the same fish that nibbled our feet when we played in the shallows.

They buried the yellow man in my uncle's experimental field. Shelly and I had helped to plant corn there with our cousins, one of us making a hole with a stake, the other following behind and dropping in the kernels. Now the corn was up to our knees. The men dug a hole in an open corner of the field. They lowered the body into it on the canvas sheet. Some of the women crossed themselves. Then the men patted down the soil and marked the grave with a stick. Afterwards everyone milled around and exchanged theories about who the dead man was and what had happened. A drug deal gone bad, people thought. Maybe an escaped convict.

I was seven, Shelly five, when we spent five months in the village of San Antonio, Belize. The year was 1974. My mother had been there before, during the summers that Shelly and I spent with our father. My uncle, her older brother, was doing research on Mayan agriculture and she'd helped construct and plant his experimental raised-field system.

Little is conventional about my mother. Before I was a year old she'd taken me to a march on Washington to protest the war in Vietnam. By the time I was in second grade and Shelly in kindergarten, we'd stayed in a Canadian commune, an apartment in Greenwich Village, a tree house, a tepee and a white Dodge van named Hippo. My mother thought nothing of taking us out of school to go to Belize for the winter.

What I remember of this time lodged itself in my mind without the help of a journal. At seven I still had trouble writing my last name; it would never have occurred to me then to try to burn a moment into my memory, to catalog events. What I remember is free of logic and of chronology. I remember that my uncle and his family were with us for Christmas, that we decorated a tree branch with red construction paper, that my aunt made donuts. In February, at Carnaval, young men with their faces covered in charcoal and sacking ran through the village throwing stones. In April, Shelly had a birthday party and cracked her piñata open with a stout stick.

San Antonio was a grid of dirt roads lined with small, whitewashed houses. The river, the Rio Hondo, ran along the east side and jungle bordered the rest. My uncle's field stood at the south end. To walk home from the field, Shelly and I took a path through the jungle, where we sometimes saw leaf-cutter ants, each hefting a scrap of bright green. Out in the sunlit front yards little boys stood in their underpants and waved machetes as tall as they were. Behind the houses women in bright cotton dresses hung laundry out to dry by size, the underthings always farthest from the street. Inside, some of the houses had pages of magazines plastered up for wallpaper. Our friend Ruby lived near the south end of town, in a house with faded turquoise trim and a yard full of red hibiscus.

Up a low hill sat the general store where you could buy bottles of Coke and orange Fanta, cans of sweetened condensed milk, green mosquito coils, girls' frilled underpants with the days of the week embroidered on the bottom, pigs' tails cured in brine. Below the store, to the right, was the ferry across the Rio Hondo. It ran on underwater cables and had to be cranked by hand. In the shallows by the ferry dock we trapped minnows in empty liquor bottles baited with raw tortilla.

To the north of the store was the schoolhouse, the largest building in San Antonio. Bats nested under the eaves, and I had seen boys knock them down with broomsticks and beat them to death. Further along, to the left, stood the house of Doña Dominga, who made a candy called *coco brut*, which she sold from her living room. At the end of her street we had once watched a man process *chicle*, gum gathered from trees in the jungle. He cooked it outside in a huge pot, stirring it with a wooden paddle. Down a low hill, in the opposite direction, was our house, the last before the river.

The house we stayed in had been made for the schoolteacher. It became vacant when he built his own just across the street, a modern building with cement block walls and a tin roof. The old house stood on stilts. It had an old-fashioned palm roof that let in the breeze: My mother said it was like sleeping in a tree. On hot days the schoolteacher's wife would come over to sit on the steps with us and list the disadvantages of a tin roof: hot in the sun, noisy in the rain. Our roof never leaked, even during the rainy season when mud washed through the streets in waves and people ran about with pieces of cardboard held over their heads.

Nearly everyone in San Antonio kept pigs. In the morning we'd see blood on the pigs' ears where vampire bats had fed during the night; everyone slept with their windows closed. The pigs at our end of the village ran loose during the day, rooting through the garbage and corn husks in the gutters along the street and getting into people's gardens. At night, and in the heat of the day, they slept under our house, the only one on stilts in that part of the village. We could hear them snuffle and grunt below us. Shelly and I came in one day and found our cousin Cedric lying face down on the floor. He'd found a knothole and was peeing through it. We were thrilled: The path to the outhouse was overgrown and I had seen snakes there and once, I swear, a bumblebee the size of my fist. Why use the outhouse when we could pee through the floor? Our mother put an end to this plan.

The house had two rooms, furnished almost entirely with hammocks. From the start I loved the feeling of being suspended and at the same time held tight. At night we lit the brittle, dark green mosquito coils under our hammocks. You balanced each coil on a little metal stand and lit the outside end with a match. They burned for about eight hours with a strong, unpleasant smoke designed to drive away mosquitoes. In the morning there'd be circles of gray ash on the plank floor. When the floor got dusty we washed it down with water Shelly and I carried from the river in red and blue plastic buckets, proud that we could carry two at a time.

The muddy green Rio Hondo was slow moving, with trees and vines draped over its banks. We bathed in it near our house, where a clearing along the bank led down to the remains of an old dock, slippery with river slime. Shelly and I were the only ones in the village with bathing suits. The boys swam at a dock by the ferry, in shorts, and the girls wore old cotton dresses. Further along the bank, under a huge tree, the girls showed us a deposit of green clay they used on their hair. You scooped out a handful and rubbed it on; it made your hair soft and slick. Around the swimming hole grew "sensitive plant," a low plant with mimosalike leaves that shrank and wilted when you touched them. A few minutes later it came back to life. I used to sit on the bank, water running off my braids, brushing my fingers over the leaves.

We ate with my mother's friends, Froylan and Balbina. Balbina had a wide face and dark, glossy hair that she kept short in front and long in the back, so that her face was fringed with curls. She wore flowered dresses over her soft, rounded body. Froylan was lean and wiry. They had three children: Maely, a son, who was a year younger than I was, and two daughters, Teti and Mirna. Their house had two rooms, a dirt floor, a thatched roof and a yard with custard apple trees.

The door that looked into the backyard was always open; chickens and sometimes a pig would wander in to look for food. Just behind the house stood the thatched cooking shed where Balbina made tortillas, taking a ball of corn dough and patting it, over and over, between two pieces of plastic bag. The corn had a dry, almost chalky smell. Balbina cooked the tortillas on a round sheet of blackened steel set over the fire pit. When the first side was done she flipped the tortilla neatly with her bare fingers.

We ate rice and beans. We ate this for breakfast, lunch and dinner. Sometimes there was an egg, sometimes Froylan brought fish from the river. The fish were called *bocas grandes*, "big mouths," and Balbina fried them till they were crisp, and served them with rice and beans. Shelly and I craved anything that wasn't rice and beans. The general store stocked cans of Campbell's Alphabet Soup and boxes of corn flakes, and sometimes, as a special treat, our mother bought us some. We ate the corn flakes in handfuls, without milk, and could go through an entire box in half an hour. Shelly also liked sweetened condensed milk, which she drank directly from the can, tipping it up against her nose.

We walked to school with Maely after breakfast, barefoot but with neatly combed hair. Kindergarten, first and second grades met in a whitewashed room with the same teacher, round Don Carmen. The day began with the ringing of the huge bell in the school yard. We found our places at the low wooden desks, then stood together to recite the Lord's Prayer. If not for my time in Belize I would never have learned it, and although my Spanish faded, it has stuck firmly in my mind, the words inseparable from the singsong in which we all intoned them. After the Lord's Prayer we belted out the national anthem: "Oh Land of the Gods by the Carib Sea, our tran-quil haven of dem-o-cra-cy!"

English is the official language of Belize, and though everyone speaks Spanish or Mayan at home, school is taught in English. It is an English ever so slightly unfamiliar; "Don't vex me now," Don Carmen said when a student misbehaved. Or he might ask one of us to "fetch" the chalk. At home on Long Island I'd struggled hopelessly over phonetics worksheets; in Don Carmen's class, because of my English, I was the star pupil. It was in Belize that I finally learned to read.

The texts were Dick and Jane primers, yellow and cracked. In

San Antonio, Dick and Jane read like fantasy. Spot, their pet, bore no resemblance to the lean, mangy dogs with narrow faces who fought and copulated in the dusty streets. And it was impossible to believe that Dick and Jane had ever had head lice, or used old newsprint for toilet paper, or been struck with a ruler. Don Carmen's corporal punishment, if the class grew noisy, consisted of going around the room with a ruler, making us stand and slapping each of us on the palm; the slap was called a "cookie." This was a joke by San Antonio standards, where fathers used belts to discipline their children. But I was so scared the first time I held out my palm that when I sat down I missed the chair, landed hard on the concrete floor and began to cry.

The village ran on sugarcane. At five in the morning when the cane trucks rattled down the hill and turned onto the road near our house, Shelly and I would wake in the dark to see their headlights slide along the walls. During the day, while Shelly, Maely and I copied Don Carmen's handwriting off the blackboard and Balbina washed laundry and made tortillas, Froylan worked in the cane fields. The price of sugar had shot up and all the young men and some of the old ones had switched from farming corn to cane. They worked land that they carved out of the jungle and leased from the government for a few pennies a hectare. The cut cane went to the sugar refinery in nearby Orange Walk. There are two ways to harvest sugarcane: You can cut it green, or you can burn the field first to scare off the snakes and get rid of the dead leaf. If you burn cane it goes sour quickly, so it needs to be rushed to the refinery before it spoils.

There were few vehicles in San Antonio: a military jeep, Don Roque's tractor, my uncle's red Volkswagen. The men who owned cane trucks took lavish care of them. Each truck had a name. My mother painted a singing bird on the door of one called the Troubadour. They came through town loaded with cane and chased by a gang of children. Sugarcane looks like bamboo. The inside is white and fibrous and sweet. We once passed a loaded cane truck parked in front of the school and Shelly grabbed one of the ropes, clambered up to the top and began throwing canes down to the rest of us.

When Froylan came home from cutting burned cane, the sweet smell of it hung on his blackened clothes. He bathed in a washtub in water Balbina heated pan by pan on her outside fire. Then each of the children bathed in fresh water, then Balbina. Everyone changed into clean clothes, Balbina and the two girls into dresses, with fresh ribbons in their neatly braided hair, and Froylan and Maely into white shirts and dark pants. Dressed to the nines, everyone in San Antonio took a stroll. Even the baby girls had gold earrings and ribbons in their hair. We walked down the street toward the school, stopping to nod or talk to friends. Tight clusters of girls in bright dresses giggled past us. In the distance we might hear "Tears on my pill-ow, pain in my heart, caused by you," sung by the groups of young men who lounged in front of the general store after it had closed, smoking cigarettes while the sunset turned to dusk.

At the small store by the river Señora Bobadia sold cubes of frozen sugar water, colored red, orange, blue and green, called "Ideals."

These came in a clear plastic wrapper which you chewed open to get at the sweetened ice. All the colors tasted exactly the same, a sweet, faintly chemical taste. On the day we got our ears pierced we were allowed two Ideals each. We took them to old Doña Donatila's house and held them against our ears until the skin went numb. Doña Donatila was a tiny, toothless woman with a tenacious grip. She poked a threaded needle through our ears and tied the thread into loops. Shelly didn't cry at all. On the way home we ate our softened Ideals, our hands reaching up of their own accord to touch our cold ears. We left the loops of white thread in our ears for two weeks, turning them twice a day. My first real earrings were a tiny pair of straw sandals, painted pink, that my mother bought in Orange Walk.

After my uncle and his family returned to Minnesota for the spring semester, my mother worked in the cane fields. She was the only woman who did, except for the occasional wife or daughter who helped out for an afternoon. My mother got up before dawn and waited by the general store with the other workers for a cane truck to come by. Whoever had rented a truck and needed to get cane in that day would pay to have it cut and loaded. My mother started out cutting cane but eventually switched to loading it. She stood on a board over the back wheel of the truck and passed great bundles over her head. Sometimes, she told me, there'd be ants swarming on the cane. She made maybe six dollars a week. Now, when I ask her why she did it, she shrugs. "I wanted to make a little money. I wanted to see what it was like."

No one had much money in San Antonio. Two families were rich enough to own generators. There was one television, run off one of the generators. It belonged to the Castillo family, and they watched it religiously in spite of the fact that the picture on the screen was barely visible. Froylan and Balbina refused to take anything my mother gave them toward food. One night as they sat around the table in the lamplight, my mother slipped a twenty-dollar bill into Balbina's hand. They sat and talked, and later the three of them walked down the hill to visit friends. While they walked, Balbina, unaware of what it was, absentmindedly shredded the paper; the scraps dropped from her hand and fell to the ground, leaving a trail like a line of leaf-cutter ants. Twenty dollars was a shocking amount of money and Balbina was scandalized. Later it became a great joke and the mention of it would make all three laugh uproariously.

We went to Orange Walk with Balbina a few weeks before Easter. Balbina was there to buy Easter dresses for Mirna and Teti, and we followed her into shops packed tight with children's white dresses, bolts of red velvet, display cases overflowing with lace and ribbons. Balbina wore her leather shoes with the raised heels. She bartered fervently in her soft Spanish. Shelly and I had never had new clothes for Easter before, but our mother let us pick out matching dresses with short, tightly pleated skirts and lace on the bodices. In another store we got new earrings, gold hoops with three gold beads. Later, the gold paint wore away and the beads turned the milky white of sugar candy that's been sucked on.

Outside, the sun was very bright. Along the sides of the wide, dirty street people hawked tamales and shaved ice from colored carts. My mother bought an orange, cut in half and sprinkled with salt. On one corner an old woman without teeth sat by a pile of oranges, which she peeled on a dented, treadle-worked machine. A stake skewered the orange and a blade peeled it concentrically; the bright rind snaked to the ground.

That evening we went to a circus. Around us crowded women with children on their hips and men who smelled of cane smoke. Two clowns came out from behind the striped curtain with an antique camera, and a trained donkey answered questions from the audience by pawing the ground with his hoof. A woman in a short skirt twirled eleven hula hoops at once, on different parts of her body.

The finale began with a small box in the center of the make-shift stage. The lights dimmed and the audience grew quiet. Then a spotlight shone on a human hand, rising out of the box. It was a small hand, pinkish brown. Another hand followed, then a head, and then a whole girl appeared, swelling out of the glass box like an expanding sponge. She wore a blue leotard and her hair was pulled back in a tight braid tied with a blue ribbon. She stood without smiling, then made a low bow that became a somersault and then a series of rippling rolls. Next she stretched on her stomach on the spangled cloth and slowly lifted her feet and legs, until she was curled in a circle, holding her ankles with her hands and staring out between her legs into the crowd. Shifting the weight to her feet, she rolled herself upright, still with that blank look, and turned her back to us. There was a rose I hadn't noticed before at her heels.

She tilted her head back and began to bend, until she was staring at us upside down. I remember the way her black braid slithered down her blue leotard and down her legs and finally hit the floor. And I remember seeing her teeth appear, bright and unexpected, to bite the stem of the rose.

On Palm Sunday Shelly and I wore our new dresses to watch the procession of the Virgin around the village. The women wore flowered hats; the men's white shirts shone in the sun. Shelly and I followed the crowd to church. The church was at the other end of the village, a long, whitewashed building with a wooden roof. Palm fronds and flowers lined the path to the door. Inside, the church was hushed and cool, lit by the high windows and the candles on the floor where Jesus Christ lay, nailed to the cross. His wooden body was gruesomely pale, except where blood darkened his wounds. Shelly and I waited in the doorway, holding hands. We watched Balbina, and then we approached together and placed our sweaty coins in the collection tray, and bent to kiss his cold feet.

My mother had been working in the cane fields for about a month when she turned yellow. This was just after the dead man turned up in the Rio Hondo; people teased her, saying he must have been a relative. Her arms were yellow, her legs, her belly, her face, even the whites of her eyes. She crawled into her hammock and stayed there. Shelly and I brought her bottles of fresh water. Balbina placed steaming bowls of chicken broth into our hands and we carried them carefully down the hill to our house. "It's hepatitis," our mother told us. But though neither Shelly nor I said a word, we were thinking the same thing: She had turned the color of the only dead person we'd ever seen.

Eventually, my grandmother in New York found out that my mother was sick. There were no telephones in San Antonio and no real way to reach someone in an emergency. My grandmother got on a plane, flew to Miami, changed to another plane. She flew into Belize back when the landing strip for an international flight was a clearing in the jungle. The airport was a two-room building where customs officers in khaki uniforms opened her bags and poked through them, then nodded. My grandmother rode in the back of an army truck over bumpy dirt roads, past trees hung with vines. She arrived at San Antonio in one of the cane trucks and took the ferry across the river. A group of people stood at the ferry dock, waiting to cross, and my grandmother accosted them. "I'm looking for my daughter, Jennifer. Where is Jennifer?" They smiled back at her. "Ah, su hija! Yeni!" They pointed up the Rio Hondo. "She's out swimming in the river."

Nostalgia is a funny thing. I remember vividly the very air of San Antonio, the warm, sweet, almost rotten smell of the river and the jungle, the feel of green clay between my fingers. I remember the taste of ripe guava and the taste of guava not quite ripe but eaten anyway. I remember all the words to "Springtime in the Rockies," a sentimental song our friend Lohinos played, the light of the kerosene lantern shining on his polished guitar. Everything from the language to the air was new to me, and so I noticed everything, without knowing I noticed it. I learned to see the way I learned Spanish, unaware, and it was in Belize that I learned it.

Now, twenty-two years later, I travel when I can, looking for amazement, for a girl in a blue leotard who seems to have no bones, for plants that wilt at the touch of a finger and then come back to life. Those months in Belize were among the most vivid in my life and I remember them with an ache of longing. But at the time it was a world too raw, too strong for me. And when my mother announced the following year that we were returning to San Antonio, I shook my eight-year-old head and refused to go.

Paola Bilbrough

Canvastown

paola bilbrough

Canvastown

That spring we lived in Canvastown
there were mushrooms the size
of dinner plates in the fields,
frayed at the gills with lice.
My mother wore a feather in her hair,
naked in profile, always painting.
My father, stringy ponytail,
pink shirt, threw pots in a cow shed.
I wanted to be the neighbour's child.

She, fat and breathless, would seat me
on top of their enormous freezer,
a mortuary of animal carcasses, feed me

bright yellow pickle, doughy bread.
The odour of basset hounds,
mutton gristle and hot vinyl.
She created nothing, sat indoors eating
melted cheese from a dented frying pan.

Furrows on her husband's brow
plowed deep, skin red as raw beef.
He could listen with the trees,
make a willow stick dance
to the song of an underground stream.
The flick of my mother's brush on canvas,
buzz of mason bees building clay houses,
the dull roar of my father's kiln.
Across the road, the weaver at his loom,
weaving a poltergeist's footfalls into a vermilion carpet.
Sound gradually drinking in all its listeners.

The fat woman and I didn't listen.
She was bored with the water diviner.
Resplendent in a green chenille housecoat,
she turned afternoon into evening
by watching *Bewitched* on TV.
I liked to lie in her overgrown garden,
watch crab apples pull malevolent
faces from the tree, poke out
their wormy tongues at passersby.

Appetites

Sara said her father had been a thief;
she remembered other people's fruit
lighting up the bushes, oranges like planets,

old sweet apples falling into her father's
flour-bag shirt. She ate nasturtiums,
waxy honey. Sugar was forbidden.

Dan would gut Sunday loaves,
the colour and texture of kapok.
After school, mouth stained green;

jelly crystals straight from the packet.
Every night chocolate pudding
thick and dark as estuary mud flats.

He had a milk run, drank from
scratched glass bottles, cream coating
his throat when he swallowed.

Sara was allowed goat's milk,
thistle milk, any milk but cow's.
That's what separated them, she said,

his complacent suburban appetites.
She thought of milk from the top of the bottle
as she fingered the satin skin of his inside wrist.

Kanji

My father and I slept in a Japanese car case,
kanji printed on the wall
in place of family portraits.
Nights I lay awake,
the black characters assumed flesh.
Clothes rustling as they changed posture.

Every morning a walk through macrocarpa
to a household of stained armrests,
chapatis and chipped enamel mugs.
Only chopsticks lay in our drawers,
Hand-whittled and oiled.

In spring we made elderflower
lemonade, white star flowers
fizzing to the surface.
The elderflower a witch among trees,
its character more disturbing than
the kanji on our walls.
A tree whose shadow could make
the mind curdle like milk.

In summer, cherry wine:
each of us scrubbed calloused heels,
crushed fruit in the belly of the bath,
feet beating out a warlike rhythm.
A dense, sweet, almost rotten smell.
Legs covered with red-black juice,
the blood of summer.

Membrane

1.
I was a festival child.
Cherry picking season
we endured unwashed hair, scant meals.

My father was a puppeteer,
I remember sunken eyes,
bruised cheeks, empty glove bodies.

In the front row of Punch and Judy
I held a stranger's baby,
its heartbeat filling the whole head.

The fontanel before
the bones knit:
a frog's throat as it swallows.

Dancers knotted up
baling twine hair. Rain.
And mud warm between the toes.

Seven-year-old skin
gossamer between myself
and the world.

In Dublin, your mother
cooked Sunday roast,
her stretch-suit vivid hydrangea pink.

Your father argued about the Pope
over tea. All I knew of Ireland
was our plow horse, Connemara.

2.
Rain, pale Irish skin,
the band screaming
"Insane in the membrane . . . "

You call me "Homegirl"
America spread
over you like fake tan.

I want to take your head,
smooth it off
with impatient thumb.

Later, the sheet curls from
a stained mattress. Your bones
move apart sounding of a forest.

Trying to sleep
in a fluorescent-lit garage,
each of us consumed by separate pasts.

Tepee

I wore only a tight necklace,
shoes the colour of a rabbit's
inside ear, buttoned over instep.

Sometimes a painted apron
with flowers unfurling,
spark-eyed heads in profile.

I carried my father's offerings:
pallid, hasty omelets
my mother would not touch,

lemon and mint
she drank in noisy gulps,
painting in the midday sun.

Clay-smudged,
I sat in a manuka tepee.
Voices in my skull, boats bobbing on a river.

When my father left, we made gingerbread people,
molasses-dark and crumbling,
ate them slowly; an arm or leg, week by week.

I wore my shoes to bed,
fell asleep to the noise of hens
roosting in the pear tree.

I dreamt my mother was a statue,
that I followed her to all the world's
cities, watched her in piazzas,

pigeons pecking grain
from her naked shoulders.
Nearby, an old violinist whose music I couldn't hear.

Rain Grimes

Fear of a Bagged Lunch

rain grimes

I was born on the kitchen table. A midwife and my dad comprised the entire birthing team. My pacifist, Joni-Mitchell-singing, vegetarian-to-the-core, "who needs shampoo?" parents did not even briefly consider the sterile experience of a hospital birth. When I finally let go of the embarrassment of that beginning enough to admit it to people, the story always elicited the same response: a wrinkle of the nose and the inevitable question "And you still ate on the table?" It was a glorious moment for my parents, that October day in 1972, when they gave birth to their very own flower child.

That kitchen table stood in a tiny cabin with no bathroom in rural Pennsylvania. My parents were both twenty-five and growing most of their own food, raising goats and making their own dairy products. I slept with my parents until I was five, drank goat's milk and peed in an outhouse, blissfully unaware that the rest of the country didn't live that way. Every photo of me shows a naked girl-child, sometimes with diaper, sometimes without, smudged with dirt and smiling like crazy. There are photos of me naked in tire swings, naked and spread-eagle in old stuffed chairs, naked and sitting on the dirty floor of our little house. One baby photo in particular was so embarrassing later that I went to great pains to hide it from my friends: I'm sitting on a pile of hay, one of my ears pierced, my smiling face exceptionally dirty, my hair a victim to home haircuts, and my cloth diaper so full it's falling off my body. No pink velvet dresses and K-Mart balloon backdrops for my family.

When I was a year and a half, my parents loaded everything we owned, which wasn't much, into a green 1952 Chevy truck and moved across the country to Washington State. My dad had built a miniature house on the back of the truck, and into this they packed our meager possessions, our two dogs and our goat Polly. (After a great deal of arguing my dad finally convinced my mom that there wasn't room for her beloved chickens.) This picking up and moving across the country was a trend that was to continue throughout my young girlhood—a family tradition, of sorts.

Moving is easy when you own almost nothing, and even easier if the things you own are so battered that they become impervious to damage. Everything we possessed had been made by one of my parents or bought secondhand from Goodwill. When I wanted something we couldn't afford (which was most of the time), my parents would do their best to build or sew it. I lusted after pin-striped jeans in third grade, and my mom valiantly sewed me stiff, ill-fitting pink denim jeans (which proceeded to fall off during a ferocious game of Red Rover). The year that Care Bears were in vogue, my brother and I received the homemade version. My mom was at a loss, luckily, when Cabbage Patch dolls hit the scene. My brother and I wanted bunk beds, and my dad promptly built them. My first bike was a hot pink number with a banana boat seat purchased at the local flea market. We got our first TV from a junk shop when I was twelve. It took me a long time to figure out that we were one step removed from the "normal" consumer chain—and that it was both a financial necessity and a conscious ideological choice for my parents.

We lived my parents' hippie dream in various New Age communities in Washington's Skagit Valley and, later, in Sedona, Arizona. When I was six, we traveled across the country again, this time to Ithaca, New York, in a red Dodge van. Yet again my dad had masterminded his version of a hippie U-Haul camper and built a wooden sleeping platform in the back of the van. We spent our nights snuggled together on the platform under our one goosedown sleeping bag, looking at the stars out the van window and reading *The Chronicles of Narnia* over and over again.

Life progressed in a similar fashion—traveling cross-country, sleeping with my parents, being naked much of the time. In Ithaca we lived in another cabin in the woods with no running water. I played in the creek, dodged the mice in our cabin, and passed countless hours melting crayons onto our wood stove. When I entered school in Ithaca, I went to an "alternative" one called Hickory Hollow three bus rides away from our home. My parents subscribed to a theory of education that did not involve being forced to learn things that I wasn't "ready" to learn—an interesting, if at times impractical, concept. When I expressed my aversion to math to my first-grade teacher, she replied that I didn't have to do my math homework if I didn't want to—instead, why didn't I go play in the corner in the fake tepee? Years later my seventh-grade teacher would wonder why I still didn't know my multiplication tables.

Being a hippie kid always marked me as different. My family's food choices were no exception. I was on the bus to Hickory Hollow with the kids from the local high school when it happened: my first public embarrassment over hippie food. My lunch box collapsed and out exploded oh-horrible-hippie-world-nonfat-plain-organic-goat's-milk yogurt, covering the aisle of the bus, splashing onto the seats and me. And as I stood there, in my puffy green Goodwill coat and holey tights and little patchwork skirt, yogurt all over my shoes, the faces of horrified high schoolers gaped at me like I was an exotic bug. Perhaps other kids didn't get yogurt in their lunch boxes—and if they did, it came in neat little plastic containers with cute foil lids and fruit on the bottom. This is the first time I can recall being conscious of my differences from other kids—and the moment when the protective bubble surrounding my idealized hippie kid existence first burst. I had been living in a sort of utopian reality, with total, guileless freedom from worry about what other people thought of me. I realized in that moment that mine was not to be a mainstream existence.

My isolation blossomed to epic proportions when we moved to Beantown, Wisconsin. My parents had two folk musician friends there—and they wanted to start a band. We drove into Beantown in 1979 in a rusty blue Datsun wagon with, yes, duct tape holding on one of the fenders. We parked it in front of our friends' house and camped out with them for some time. It seemed like months to my seven-year-old mind, and perhaps it was. However long, it was enough to bring the Beantown police to the door of the house, asking about the strange, vagrant car parked on the street. That visit from the police is cemented in my memory as my family's initiation into our brand new identity as the town freaks. Did "normal" people have the police coming to their door because their car looked so dilapidated? Somehow, I didn't think so.

The vortex of the small-town Midwest sucked us in and held us captive for thirteen long years. There in the vortex, all the things about us that hadn't seemed that strange before took on a whole new meaning. We were a complete anomaly to the residents of this tiny town. The people of Beantown must have been vaguely aware that the hippie culture existed, but it rarely, if ever, infiltrated their stable community. Other than my parents' band mates, we stood alone on an island of hippie weirdness, or at least so it seemed to me at that young age when every difference is magnified. We were almost the only vegetarians in town. My parents were folk musicians, a virtually unheard of and severely misunderstood profession. My mom still made most of our clothes, and a wood stove was still our only source of heat. My mom wore colorful ethnic fabrics and knee-high leather boots instead of polyester pantsuits and flats. My dad bought all his clothes at the local Salvation Army, including the series of corduroy and leather vests that he remained strangely attached to even into the mid-eighties, much to my dismay. My parents weren't Christians—they were pagans, and our "bible" was a combination of the *I-Ching,* Tarot cards and the channelings of Seth. We drove a succession of rusty cars that always looked as if they couldn't make it another mile, including one of our more embarrassing vehicles, a 1965 red Plymouth Valiant. The Valiant would swing into the school parking lot to pick me up after school, looking grossly out of place next to the Ford Escorts and minivans. When viewed through the lens of mainstream culture, our hippie ways were incomprehensible. Obscure lifestyles, or any sort of difference, can seem threatening in a small town—and we were misjudged accordingly. People saw my parents and immediately assumed (incorrectly) that they did drugs. I was taunted in eighth grade, asked if my parents had seen all of the Cheech and Chong movies. There was a vaguely dangerous mystique surrounding our difference.

Being different inside our home was easier to bear than the more public differences—no one could see my dad meditating or my mom playing the dulcimer. Food continued to be the most public declaration of my family's strangeness. In my school they segregated the cold lunch kids from the hot lunch kids—and no, my mom did not allow me to eat any of the preservative-laden, non-organic foods full of processed meats and refined sugar served in my school cafeteria. I was, of course, a cold lunch kid. Which meant that I had to sit at a table in the lunch room that for some reason was perpendicular to all the rows of hot lunch tables. We, the few cold lunch kids, spent the whole hour providing an amusing visual distraction for the hot lunch kids. Our bagged lunches were of great interest to the hot lunchers—something to look at while they slurped down hot dogs and mac-n-cheese and chocolate cake and jello and hamburgers and chop suey. And my lunch was the most interesting of all. The kids had seen Velveeta and white bread and Cheetos and Capri Sun juice boxes before, but they hadn't been exposed to homemade wheat bread and blue corn chips and tofu and natural licorice. And so it happened again and again—the dreaded natural food incident. The pointing finger, the gaping mouth and the inevitable comment: "What *is* that?" How could I explain blue corn chips to kids raised on white bread? I tried to be strong—I tried to stand up for my family's organic choices, and I tried to tell them that the chips tasted good. But they were wasted words—because to them all that mattered was that the food looked different, which made it weird, which made *me* weird.

My repeated public embarrassments due to the contents of my lunch bag bred a deep resentment inside me about my family's food choices. I begged my dad to buy hot dogs. Secretly plotting which sugar cereals I could get my hands on and dreaming of Oscar Meyer bologna sandwiches on white bread with that nice bright yellow mustard, I revolted. My tolerance for their food choices hit its limit with tempeh. My mom grew tempeh in their bedroom. It smelled bad and looked worse. Their bedroom floor was covered with pans of white molding cakes, which my mom would bring downstairs, slice into neat squares, fry and serve for dinner. I would not eat tempeh.

My friends went to college and became vegetarians. I went to college and became a meat eater. After nineteen years of being force-fed tofu and beans and rice, vegetarianism did not hold an enigmatic appeal for me. Early in my freshman year a large group of my newly turned vegetarian friends discovered, to their immense joy, a restaurant that served tofu dogs. This was like the Second Coming for them. They came to my room in an excited bunch, inviting me to join them to "go out for tofu dogs." I declined. The natural foods craze held no sense of independence or contained rebellion for me. I felt more insurgent satisfaction from eating a hamburger or a slice of chocolate cake. So even now, as an adult who enjoys eating healthy foods and is surrounded by a community that sanctions rather than punishes this choice, I am still guilty of occasional secret trips to the drive-through lane of fast-food restaurants. I lust after processed sugar, red meat, full-fat dairy. It is the legacy of growing up vegetarian and sugar free, the curse of the hippie kid turned adult.

By the time I was a teenager, I had already lived as a nonconformist and, in some ways, that left me no direction to go but toward conformity. My parents had already fought many battles for me. I was so free to become who I wanted to be that I just wanted to be like everyone else. In high school, my friends rebelled against authority by stealing their parents' cigarettes, skipping class and getting stoned at lunch. I curled my bangs and became a cheerleader and class president. My classmates did Tarot cards and listened to Pink Floyd. I did my homework religiously and organized the school prom. Thankfully, my parents were patient enough to let this wild stage run its course, as I pranced through my teen years in disguise—my bangs curled high and immobilized with hair spray, my lips glimmering with shell-pink lipstick, my jeans rolled tight to my leg, my Keds whiter than white. They may have secretly lamented my embrace of the trappings of mainstream teenage life— but they never said a word.

My rebellious phase is long past; normalcy is no longer an

icon. I left the towering bangs by the wayside. More important, however, is that everything that once felt shameful now seems interesting; I actually enjoy the looks of incredulity from people who did not grow up as I did when I tell my childhood story. I'm no longer embarrassed to describe the setting of my birth—or to admit that my parents weren't married until I was seven. I beg my mom to sew me clothes, having long forgotten the trauma of the pink jeans. I humbly ask her how best to cook tofu, and don't mind that people know my dad still meditates on a nightly basis. Our family mantra, "You create your own reality," our version of the Lord's Prayer, has found its way into my daily life. I try to balance my parents' hippie values with my own brand of nineties realism and a healthy dose of ex-hippie-kid skepticism. I've stopped viewing the world through a lens that magnifies difference and makes it undesirable. And I've finally forgiven my parents for all the rusty cars and tofu sandwiches, for the homemade Care Bears and home haircuts. They knew what they were doing.

Chelsea Cain

Welcome Home

chelsea cain

The look is key—worn blue corduroys, a black cotton Indian-style shirt with ornate white piping over a black tank top, brown leather boots, long hair braided, each braid held in place with a Pocahontas-style leather lace-up tie. Sans makeup. Sans jewelry (save for beads or anything made with tiny peace signs). It's more Michelle Phillips California Hippie than Marianne Faithfull Bohemian Hippie or Grace Slick Haight-Ashbury Hippie. (There are subtle but very important differences.) I want to blend in but I don't want to be the first one arrested if the cops come.

There are ten thousand of us and we are in the open field, arms linked, chanting. We are swaying to the unrelenting heartbeat of a hundred bongo drums. It is distressingly hot and as people begin to strip so that they can dance naked in the circle, I find myself worrying about things like sunscreen and personal hygiene and body image. The air is thick with marijuana smoke and incense and body odor and I can't feel my toes because about an hour ago when a bearded man in bicycle shorts offered me tea I forgot to ask "Is this special tea?" and I drank a cup before I realized that it was laced.

So we are chanting "Om," all ten thousand of us, in the heat, packed like blinking, bewildered cows into the central meadow, and all at once everything stops and someone points to the sky. There is a hawk circling up above, to the right of the two news helicopters. "A hawk!" someone cries. "It's a blessing!" And a murmur runs through the crowd as ten thousand fingers point skyward and the hawk circles and the news helicopters close in and I realize that I can't feel my knees. The hawk disappears over the trees and the silence is broken. The hippies leap barefoot into the air, the music begins and a stranger in a tunic hugs me for no reason. If I could feel my tongue, I think, I would say something.

I had been hearing about the Rainbow Gathering for years, so when my friend Mike asked me if I wanted to go, I didn't hesitate. His girlfriend, Karen, had gone every year for seven years and Mike had attended the last two. I had heard stories of the Gathering: of pot smoking, tent sex, meadow romping and general vegetarian-earth-friendly-feel-good-love-one-another-over-a-plate-of-organic-casserole earnestness. It was, I had heard, one of the last bastions of sixties-style counterculture. The kid of hippies, I saw it as an opportunity to go home. Like my parents, these people had the true knowledge; unlike them, the Rainbows had never moved on. They were frozen, flashing a peace sign, in the Zeitgeist of 1968.

"Sure," I told Mike. "Let's go."

There is a Rainbow Gathering Web page that tells the whole story. The first Gathering was held in 1972, when twenty thousand hippies collected in the woods of Colorado to evolve, expand, harmonize, love and embrace peace. They did drugs, slept in tepees, ate millet, played music, called each other "brother" and "sister" and pledged to abandon authoritarian hierarchy, bad trips, bad vibes, bad attitudes and aggressive dogs. It was such a good time that they decided the event should occur annually, on public land, and it has been held every summer since.

In 1972, I was a naked flower baby on a farm commune in Iowa. My mother spent that summer sanding sixty years of thick white paint off the kitchen window frames. Every day she sanded that paint. It came off in thin strings and fine white dust, each layer revealing another underneath it. By fall the four frames were natural wood again and she began another project: sewing my father a green felt Robin Hood shirt (I have pictures of him smiling sheepishly in it). My parents were both on the run: my mother from society's expectations for women at the time, my father from the draft and the war machine. My memories of this period are pure and sweet: love and music, dogs and garden vegetables, sunshine and songs. People came and went. There were ten, eight, twelve at a time. They came together from different pasts, lived together for a few years, then continued on to their own remarkable, inevitable futures.

It was all magic to me. Even today I look at my early childhood as the best part of myself. It is something you can only understand if you were there. Every once in a while I'll meet someone named "Summer," or "Star," and I'll say, "Your parents were hippies, weren't they?" and she'll say, "Yeah," and I'll say, "Mine too," and we won't have to say anything more because we will understand some basic part of each other, some true thing. When I first heard about the Gathering, I expected it to be like that—a big family reunion, a living memory—something like those half-remembered evenings listening to the Dead through kitchen speakers on that Iowa farmhouse porch.

But it wasn't like that at all. Like so many holidays, the celebration itself has evolved into a celebration of a celebration rather than anything specific. A lot of the people I know who go were born after Vietnam, after Nixon, and they do not remember a time when their mothers did not shave their armpits. For them the Gathering is a chance to party naked in the woods. Yet there is also a core group of Rainbows who have been at the center of the Gathering from the beginning, who have never left this culture, who have raised their children in it, and these are the people who interest me.

This year's Gathering took place in the high desert of central Oregon, where the only trees are ponderosa pines and you half expect Pa Cartwright and his boys to come galloping over the horizon looking for lost steers. All that preceding week I had been watching the local Portland news air dispatches from Prineville, a town of six thousand and the closest to the Gathering site. The good townspeople were in a twitter, awaiting the caravans of old VW buses like farmers listening for the telltale hum of approaching locusts. A stern Prineville PD representative warned that loitering was already on the rise.

Mike and Karen arrived at my Portland apartment with a

car full of supplies and a Dead sticker on the back window. We decided to take separate vehicles to the site—they were being vague about when they wanted to leave, and I didn't want to be stranded should I become hysterical and need to watch TV or something. The plan was to stay up there a week. Seven days. In the woods. With no electricity, shower, modem, telephone or permanent waterproof shelter. "You have camped before, right?" asked Mike.

"Sure," I said. And I had, when I was nine, with my mom, for a couple of days. Now I was committed to a whole week of living off the land in a national forest, and I didn't even own a backpack. I borrowed one from my grandmother—a bright red nylon backpack. My aunt, apparently more worried that I might catch cold than freak out on bad acid or get dysentery, lent me a bright red down-filled ski cap, rain pants, a rain slicker, gloves and two sets of polythermal long johns. If I wore it all I would look like a stylish Smurf.

We drove from Portland to the Gathering in just under five hours, taking turns as the lead car so as to be antiauthoritarian and avoid any semblance of hierarchy. Just past Prineville, I followed them off the paved road at a sign with a crudely drawn heart on it that read "Welcome home," and continued down a gravel road, passing a couple of grinning drivers who flashed me peace signs.

As we approached the site entrance we were greeted by waving, leaping hippies who cried out "Welcome home!" They motioned for us to stop, and a dreadlocked middle-aged woman in a short floral-print dress came bounding over to Mike's car. I watched as she gave him a big hug and instructions and then skipped over to me.

Chelsea Cain ⭐ 109

"Hi!" she said. "Welcome home, sister! I love you!" She reached in and gave me a tight, sweaty squeeze. "You're beautiful. We're glad you're here. Just follow your friend to parking lot number eight." She waved me along and then went bounding over to the next car. I followed Mike, who was following pointing hippies, to a large meadow filled with cars. We were both directed where to park and proceeded to unload the gear and hoist it on our backs. With my heavy pack strapped with a sleeping bag, sleeping roll, water jug and two coats, it was all I could do to remain vertical. I joined Mike and Karen who were similarly encumbered, and the three of us started stumbling down the dusty dirt road with the steady march of long-haired campers. Grateful Dead music wafted through the pines, a steady ambient noise that would float disembodied through the entire site.

After a quarter-mile hike we reached the shuttle, an old VW bus that, when it wasn't providing rides, was somebody's home. A jagged square hole had been hand-cut in the roof so passengers could crawl up on top of the bus to a makeshift deck. Inside, the walls were littered with Dead show ticket stubs and Legalize Hemp slogans. The driver, a scruffy, leather-vested man in his forties, took our packs and stacked them on a rack outside the back of the bus. After our packs were secured, we piled in, one after another, man, woman, child, dog, until there were twenty-six of us, not counting the canines and the ten or twelve people who rode upstairs. It was hot and we were all sweating from the hike from the parking lot, but spirits were high—as was the driver.

We rattled along dirt roads for five miles, and with each turn in the road the bus seemed to lurch to one side and then rock back a second, before settling on four tires.

"I was in a bus that rolled once," a woman standing next to me said to no one in particular. She was wearing a white tank top without a bra and her huge breasts swung in wide arcs with each turn of the vehicle.

Another woman called to the driver and he stopped to wait for her. She opened the side door and the bus was flooded with a brief blast of fresh air. "Thanks, brother," she said to the driver. "I baked a pie for Badger's wedding and I gotta get on site."

We passed other meadows filled with cars: Bus Village, where all the "live in" vehicles park, and Bus Village II. Finally we got to Welcome Home, the entrance to Downtown, and the shuttle pulled to a stop.

"Zuzus [treats, as in cookies or candy] and tips would be appreciated, brothers and sisters," the driver announced as we unloaded. "Especially green herb."

Mike and Karen and I strapped on our gear again. On the way past the bus driver Karen stopped to give him two pieces of bread, and I gave him a pecan sticky bun purchased in Portland that morning. He seemed pleased, more with the bread than with the sticky bun. What takes on value at a Gathering, I will learn, is not always what is prized in Babylon.

When we arrived that afternoon, there were already twelve thousand people, with a rumored three hundred more arriving every hour. The trails were like city streets, except that all the people smile and wave at you. We walked past the welcome site and through the trading circle, past the Hare Krishna tent, the Jesus tent, the Lost and Found, the information booth, and up toward

Morning Star Kitchen where we found a place to pitch our tents.

The Gatherings are remarkably well organized. Locations are thoroughly scouted and then a few hundred people come early for "seed week," when the main structures are built. Oil drums are buried in mud with fires underneath to make ovens, shitters are dug, fire pits are lined with stones and surrounded with log benches, tents are erected, stages are built, signs are posted, paths are worn, even a sweathouse is constructed. These people know what they are doing. Many have been doing it for twenty years. Karen told me that most of the old Rainbows she knows organize their whole lives around the event, living in their vans, taking odd jobs, traveling from Gathering to Gathering. Someday, a banner near our campsite read, We Will Gather 4 Ever.

After unpacking our gear, Mike and Karen and I hiked up through Tepee Village past the main meadow to a coffee circle kitchen called Lovin' Ovens (all the kitchens had names: Morning Star, Turtle Island and so on) where some sort of celebration was going on.

Badger's wedding! I remembered the sister with the pie on the bus. Here he was, a stocky, grinning man in his forties dressed in dirty jeans with a wide belt, wearing boots, a thick long-sleeved shirt and a wide-brimmed leather hat. His bride was in her forties, too, short, with curly black hair tied back with an ornate clip, and wearing a long colorfully embroidered Nepali dress. They embraced and the circle of people around them began to Om until the sound rose to a crescendo and broke and everyone cheered.

Guitars started up and the crowd began to dance and twirl to Dead standards. Mike and Karen disappeared to say hello to someone they knew from the previous year, so I sat back on the log where I was perched and took in the scene. Everyone was having such a good time. It was Woodstock, without the music, the rain or the war.

I felt a tap on my shoulder and turned expecting to see Mike or Karen. Instead, a young man gazed at me with glazed eyes. "Hey sister," he said. "I'm giving out random massages. You want one?"

"Sure," I said, practicing being free-spirited and spontaneous.

"Come lay down on my blanket," the young brother said, and I followed him back into the main meadow where he had laid down a blanket in the tall grass. He told me his name was Lizard.

I spread out on my belly on the blanket and Lizard unsnapped my overall straps and folded them back so my tank top was exposed. He started kneading my shoulders, then my back, arms and legs. After a while he had me flip over on my back, then he folded down my overalls, lifted up my tank top and began to massage my bare stomach.

This is so great, I thought. It is so great that two strangers of the opposite sex can have this random totally nonsexual encounter without any of society's hang-ups or expectations.

"Now this is the part where you have to tell me if I make you uncomfortable," Lizard said. He began to massage my legs, creeping slowly up my inner thighs.

Was he molesting me, or just being thorough?

"Just tell me if I make you uncomfortable," he said again.

His kneading fingers crept higher and higher.

"Um, Lizard?"

"Stop?"

"Stop."

I sat up on the blanket and thanked him for the massage but explained that it had become imperative that I find my friends immediately as they might be missing me by now.

"Plant one here, sister," he said, pointing at his puckered lips.

I gave him a fleeting peck on his pucker, managing to avoid the tongue he tried to slip into my mouth.

By the time I got back to the wedding, Mike and Karen were nowhere to be found, but I could see that the minions were gathering in the main meadow for dinner circle and I figured that's where I'd find them. I headed down the trail, passing Lizard leading another sister to his blanket boudoir.

I found Mike amid the six thousand people who had dinner that night (Karen had volunteered to hand out bread). We all listened to announcements no one could hear because "megaphones would be a power trip." Then everyone rose, joined hands and Omed for a few minutes. Finally we all formed huge concentric circles and kitchen workers came around giving each waiting bowl a healthy scoop of rice and beans served out of dirty red-and-white coolers. The mothers, children and pregnant sisters got fed first, taking a good half of the food supply, then everyone else got what was left over. Considering that your portion depended on where you happened to be sitting when the cooler ran out, people were surprisingly mellow, content to get even one helping. After dinner, the magic hat came around and we were encouraged to put a few cents in if we could spare it. The hat money goes for food and coffee, with a guarantee that not a cent will be spent on Rainbow vices such as meat, nicotine or alcohol—though it is common knowledge that the kitchen workers get free drugs, a pretty serious incentive to sign up for dish duty.

There is plenty of substance use at the Gathering. Maybe 70 percent of the adults are under the influence at any given time. People smoke joints like cigarettes (which are not nearly as tolerated) and drop LSD and take mushrooms. But it is caffeine that seems to be the drug Rainbows are most enamored with.

"Is the coffee done yet, man?" I had split up with Mike and Karen after dinner and found my way back to the Lovin' Ovens fire pit. There were twenty-some hippies huddled around the fire, several clutching Starbucks travel mugs, waiting for the five-gallon coffeepot to boil. Coffee is a complicated process at the Gathering. A delicate combination of instant, freeze-dried coffee out of a can and fresh ground coffee is stirred into creek water, which is heated over an open fire for a half hour until it boils. It's cowboy coffee, swirling with debris and chunks of unidentifiable solids. It was my first glimpse of nineties culture at the Gathering—everyone around the fire was dying for a good cappuccino.

I headed back to my tent after my cup, and got a surprisingly good night's sleep. When I woke up, I joined Mike and Karen for fried potatoes and coffee from Morning Star, and then headed for the trading circle. It was mid-morning and already hot. Women were shedding shirts to go bare-chested, and many men wore nothing but long skirts. I walked along the main trail to the circle, where people put out blankets of wares, anything from beads to clothing to marijuana.

You can't use cash in the trading circle. You have to barter for anything you want. I saw one kid who wanted a zipper he saw laid out on someone's blanket. The zipper's owner said, "What do you got to trade?" The kid thought a minute and then said, "I've got this camera." He produced the camera, and the zipper owner immediately agreed to the barter. But the kid wasn't a total push-over—he'd only trade the camera for two zippers. It was, the kid explained, a really nice camera.

The previous year, Karen told me, she traded a little piece of suede she got out of a free box at a garage sale for half an ounce of pot. "I felt sort of bad," she said. "But he really wanted it. I think he thought he got the better end of the bargain."

The Rainbow barter economy is driven by immediate gratification. Mike met a kid who traded his graduation watch for an apple. Candy bars are worth their weight in gold. I watched a woman trade the shirt off her back for a York Peppermint Patty. Pleasure is valued over utility, indulgence over practicality.

Mike had told me to bring trade fodder, and after a brief negotiation I scored thirty sticks of pachouli incense for three snack-size Hershey's bars. The pachouli sticks were wrapped in plastic and I found a place in the grass and unwrapped them, inhaling the sweet aroma. I lit a stick and stuck it in the dirt beside me and then, wheezing in its smoke, sat at the edge of the trading circle, watching all the activity. Men in loincloths, disheveled children, topless women in kerchiefs. A long-bearded man in his fifties strummed "Where have all the flowers gone?" I watched it all with awe and trepidation. I loved the sense of community. I loved the affirmation and the music and the feeling of family. These people had, at least temporarily, created a working, cash-free utopia. There was free child care, free food, free cigarettes, free drugs, free medical care, an authentic democratic system of political representation and a population that was happy and provided for.

Yet there was something disturbing about it all. The presumed familiarity I found comforting was also strangely invasive. What if you didn't want to be hugged every couple of minutes? Karen told me that every year there are four or five reported rapes (a low number given the thousands in attendance, she pointed out), which usually occur because a sister feels she "can't say no." I had kissed Lizard, hadn't I? Indeed, the Rainbow ethos is to be open, to indulge, to be free. It's a noble pursuit, especially in the context of today's society, which seems to encourage repression of these same impulses. But this "free love as emancipation" is the same old paradigm that my mother faced thirty years ago. In the end, sixties-style free love seemed to be more about men getting their penises tickled than achieving any kind of gender equity through rejecting sexual hang-ups and repression. The 1970s saw more than one woman look up from the bread she was baking to realize that she was, despite her progressive politics and lack of makeup, still in the fucking kitchen. Many of these women went on, like my mother, to cut their Joan Baez tresses and join the feminist movement. Three decades later, and the Gathering gender roles remain bizarrely traditional. The female Rainbow archetype is topless, in a long skirt, with a couple of toddlers trailing behind her. She is both a "sister" and a "mother," who can make macramé and knows the medicinal properties of herbs. Was this sexist, or was it free? I couldn't decide.

I wandered through the trading circle, past the blankets full of food, drugs, scarves, bongs, hemp necklaces, hats and more, down the main trail to the main meadow. The trail was full of campers filing past on their way to workshops (tai chi, yoga, meditation), the sweat lodge, the Church of Elvis. I joined a group of about seventy people that had gathered in a circle in the main meadow. They were, I learned, the Homeland Council, and they were meeting to discuss buying land and settling into a permanent Rainbow community. A feather was passed around the circle and whoever held it had the attention of the group. The keeper of the feather could speak as long as he or she wished and then the feather was passed to the next person who wanted it. It was a thoroughly democratic process and excruciatingly time consuming as person after person rambled on about the ills of established society. The idea, as I understand it, was to purchase a few acres, build on them, and then send the brothers to caravan around the country selling baked goods and baskets so the sisters could stay home with the babies. It's not a new dream. Over the years several tribes have splintered off from the Gathering to settle full time. There is the Krishna Tribe, the Turtle Family, the (I kid you not) Naked Tribe. These people really really do not want to participate. They are desperate for an alternative to what they see as a corrupt technological society. Yet there are conflicts to be overcome, the main one being whether or not to be "jones free." The argument against drugs is a simple one: no drugs, no cops. Allow drugs, and you ask for police attention, especially if local teens get turned on by any of the resident Rainbows. This, as you can imagine, is a big point of contention and has been a conversation stopper at the Homeland Council for the many years it has been meeting.

To their credit, the police have been remarkably tolerant of national Gathering activities. The Rainbows choose public land that is relatively out of the way, collect all the necessary permits, inform nearby towns and spend weeks after the Gathering cleaning up and planting trees. Often their presence is a boon to the local economy, as Rainbows spend thousands of dollars on supplies, from wheat flour to condoms. Yet there is a police presence. Cruisers roll through and around the camp regularly, but officers ignore most of what they see—the general rule is that if it's inside the camp boundaries, it's legal. Because the police are not a threat, passing police cars are often greeted with stoned smiles and peace signs and I saw more than one cop flash a peace sign back.

A pudgy member of the Naked Tribe approached and took a seat next to me in the grass. I managed to rescue my plastic-wrapped package just in time. "Hey, man," I said. "Watch the pachouli."

That night, at the Fourth of July Eve celebration, everyone was decked out in his or her finest Janis Joplin attire. There were big colorful hats, flowing vintage dresses, leather pants and knee-high lace-up boots. Even rumors of food poisoning and long lines at the sister shitters did not dampen the festive spirit. Spaghetti was served to almost seven thousand people at dinner and the magic hat collected over $2,500. After dinner, bonfires were lit all over the site, so that points of light flickered everywhere in the darkness. A talent show was held at Turtle Island and the kitchens were on hand with cookies and coffee. I wore an Indian-print dress over blue corduroys, a thick wool shirt and my aunt's red hat with earflaps. Luckily, the point was to look like a freak, or I might have stood out.

I left Mike and Karen at Turtle Island gathering wood for a

fire, and tried to find my way back to the tents. The drumming circles had started and the steady beating echoed from every direction. Everyone I passed greeted me with enormous smiles and hugs. (It's hard to pass a Rainbow without getting hugged and asked for the time; though most Rainbows do not wear watches on principle, they are always interested in what time it is.) I ended up completely turned around and found myself in a kitchen I had never been in before. Freezing cold and lost, I found a spot on a log and joined a group of Rainbows sitting around a small fire.

A long-haired sister strummed softly on her guitar and no one spoke, all eyes on the fire. Then another sister joined the circle with a guitar and she started to play and the first sister joined in with her guitar and soon we were all singing "Sugar Magnolia." I did not know I knew the words, but somehow they surfaced from my childhood and it occurred to me that I had sat around this fire before, a long time ago, singing the same song with people who looked not unlike these. I stayed at the fire circle for another hour singing old songs from the sixties with strangers, and then found my way to the tent where I fell asleep to the mindless throb of a hundred drum circles.

Now, the hawk. It is July 4, the apex of the celebration, and we are all standing, heads back, gazing up at the bright sky as the hawk banks and then disappears over the woods. Most of these people have been up all night, many on LSD, and they are a bit frayed. We have been silent since dawn, a tradition that culminates at noon with the children parading into the main meadow and a final Om breaking the silence. It is 12:15, and the children have already arrived, faces painted, wearing handmade costumes and carrying colorful banners and masks. They run free with the dogs. Karen is radiant in her suede boots and Charlie's Angels hair. She is in her element, surrounded by her Rainbow family. Everyone is dancing and grinning and passing around huge chunks of dripping watermelon. The hawk is a good omen, a sign that the next year will be a happy one. There is some more talk about a permanent settlement, but not much is made of it. It is a pipe dream, and no one really believes it will happen. For all their anti-establishment talk, many of the Rainbows hold down jobs. The runaways will return to their parents, or back to the streets. The college students will return to study. The core Rainbows will begin to plan next year's Gathering, of which there is already much talk, and later today I will decide to leave early and return to Portland.

I wanted to come home. But this isn't it. My parents' counterculture was reacting to a war and an establishment that had proven again and again that it could not be trusted. The Rainbow Gathering rejects society for the sake of it, because it always has. Am I a sellout because I don't want to live in a bus? Because I am typing this on a computer? Because I shave my legs?

It comes down to this: During my three days here I have been called "sister" and greeted by strangers as if we were raised in the same tepee. But they are not my family. I think that the people who love the Gatherings, who live for them, are people who don't feel that sort of adoration anywhere else. The hippie daze of my memories is gone, vanished with the era and the youth of its players. It cannot be called back and, except for a minute or two of campfire singing, it cannot be re-created.

Yet there is something going on here. Something that, if unsettling, is still admirable. The Rainbows' appeal lies in their fragile belief in the ability to create a better world. It is in their moony hopefulness, in their lack of self-consciousness, in their seeming dearth of social hang-ups. I am not a Rainbow, but it is not because I don't want to be. There is a part of me that wants to name myself Bear, buy a pottery wheel and move to the woods. There is a part of me that wants to join the Naked Tribe and get high every day and know for certain that my government does not have my best interests at heart. I long for the simple righteousness of my childhood. But I was there. For the very best of it. And because I saw it end, I know it is over.

Cecily Schmidt

Common Threads

cecily schmidt

Iowa is such subtle Beauty. I am driving east toward Cedar County, the sun glowing orange in my rearview mirror. The corn fields exude something like nobility, their crowns beginning to wither with the dignity of a very old person's hands. November touches the countryside with the honey-coated glow that is distinctly present when the sun is low in the sky. This light gets to the core. Burrowing into crevices between soybean plants, twisting up and down rows of corn, it fills entire plains with auburn fire. It seeps up under my eyelids and finds its way to my breastbone where it lingers, humming, a moment more. Dusk brings dark purple shadows to spaces where shades of earth roll into the gentle swaying slope of the Iowa horizon. I am driving under a big midwestern sky, and once again the season is about to fall.

I know it is autumn now because yesterday I awoke early, reached for the faded blue sheet that serves as my curtain and pulled it over my head to inhale the potency of morning. Across the yard, the maple tree was stained with sun. I couldn't take my eyes from the orange leaves in quiet conversation with patches of newly lit sky. It seems that blue is always listening. Lying on my stomach, my chin propped on the windowsill, gaze transfixed on the fiery maple, I was reminded of hiking through a myriad of fallen leaves as a small child, holding tightly to the hand of my father, who urged me to be quiet and listen to the swishing at our feet. I wondered then, craning my neck to see into the highest trees where the most brightly colored leaves still clung to their branches, if the brightest stars are those that are about to fall. I wondered what would happen if a strong wind came and sent those leaves tumbling on air currents changing direction as fast as my small-bodied breath.

For as long as I can remember, there has been a moment when I realize the seasons have changed. Autumn is particularly poignant. In that moment, whether twenty years ago walking through whispering leaves with my father or yesterday morning awakened by the light of the maple tree, I think of myself as a leaf, falling again, sustained by the wind's direction.

I slow down as I enter the tiny town of Springdale, scarcely more than a row of houses separated from each other by pine trees. The light has almost gone completely now, except for a random streetlight and a few early stars. I notice the first curls of smoke rising from several chimneys. I open the window and inhale the familiar smell of remembering. It is November again. I am the same age my mother was when she married my father.

In the late autumn of 1974, my parents had been married less than a year and were living in an upper flat on the east side of

Milwaukee, searching for something they could call their own. My mom was finishing school, my dad working as an adolescent care worker at the County Mental Health Center, when he learned of a related facility in Plymouth, about sixty miles north of Milwaukee. It was October when they found the farmhouse—eight miles outside of Plymouth—situated majestically atop a high hill overlooking the Kettle Moraine forest, a mosaic of crimson and gold at that season. My mom remembers the sun setting as the wheels of their tiny blue Toyota sped along Wisconsin country roads toward the next stage of their life together. She recalls how the light poured from the golden underbelly of a plum-colored sky and she knew it was where she wanted to be. They lived there for the next three years, paying $140 a month for a four bedroom house surrounded by beautiful Wisconsin farmland and forest.

That big white house in Wisconsin is where I was conceived. It was heated by the same wood stove that heated the house I moved out of, eighteen years later. Shortly after I was born in January 1976, an ice storm hit our quiet country home and we were without power for three days. My mother moved my cradle next to the potbelly stove so that I could sleep under the comforting haze of its warmth. Large pots of snow were collected and set on the stove to melt so we would have water. For three days, my parents and their tiny new life huddled around slow stew and candlelight stories.

I've heard the tale many times. I listen, still drawn to the way my mother's eyes deepen when she speaks of waking up early to find the world coated with a thick layer of glass, as if the brightest stars had indeed fallen overnight, leaving ashes softly flickering. I listen because her eyes tell me again and again that I am her daughter. In the country of memory, there is a place that resembles winter. It is here that my mother stands in front of the farmhouse, inhaling the quiet breath of snow. She does not move, for with any tiny movement the delicacy of such a starry winter morning will be shattered. The tightly wrapped bundle in her arms is me, and I am warm against her breast. She calls to a figure some distance away, but I don't know her words. This memory is silent. The figure is my father. He is scraping ice from the windshield of the car. He looks up when she calls and nods in response, taking a moment to remove his leather work gloves and blow on his numbed fingers. The gray of his stocking cap is almost imperceptible against the sky. Despite the cold, he is at ease. My mother lingers on the front step a moment longer, wondering how the brutal winds of the storm last night could result in a morning so fragile as this.

There is a photograph from my parents' days at the Wisconsin farmhouse in which my father sits in a worn-out chair, wearing rusty orange corduroys and a brown argyle sweater. His hair, uncombed and shaggy, hangs to his shoulders and his winter beard is just beginning to form. My mom is bent over him with her arms around his chest and her chin on his shoulder. Her hair is dark and rich, coming nearly to her waist. It falls over one side, framing the shared contentment in their faces. The photo was taken twenty-three years ago in the early days of November, before I was born. Behind them, the potbelly wood stove radiates warmth, making their cheeks flushed.

During their time in the country, my parents planted seeds that grew into fresh tomatoes, homemade basil pesto and a daughter who was just as nourished by the dark soil as the wild-flowers were. Listening to my parents' stories, I am filled with a strange sense that I am reliving their experience, caught on an invisible thread that winds itself in circles. I wonder if the time elapsed between generations has made it impossible to really understand each other's experience. When my parents were my age, this country was in the throes of an influential stage, with an atmosphere of experimentation and rebellion. People everywhere were questioning the basic structure against which many American standards stood.

Although my parents and I have been referred to as hippies countless times, I still don't know what the word means. It is a label spawned by popular culture during my parents' youth, but its use has persevered through my own. How can so many scattered concepts over so long breed concrete definition? Of course there is a pile of stereotypes, as with most labels used to define human beings, but my parents were not the strung-out, stoned-to-the-bone drifters on a perpetual search for the next Dead show; they were not the freaked-out screaming radicals, the starry-eyed tie-dyed dreamers or the vegetarian environmentalists whose moral purity could wound the soul. Instead, my parents were calm, quiet, creative individuals who happened to be alive during a dynamic time.

Inevitably, the period influenced the people they are. But while some people might have changed to fit the movement of the sixties and seventies, in my parents' case, the movement just seemed to fit them. If being a hippie meant wearing plaid bell-bottoms on your wedding day, sporting a dandelion instead of a corsage to the senior prom, protesting the Vietnam War, and smoking marijuana and remembering to inhale, then my parents were hippies once. If it has anything to do with honesty, compassion, appreciating the silence of a winter morning, remembering to listen when the leaves fall and believing in magic, then my parents were, and still are, hippies.

When I imagine the sixties and seventies, I am filled with a sad sense that something important has been lost—something that connected people, regardless of their many directions. Growing up in the aftermath of the "hippie movement" has fragmented youth identity. We are propelled headlong into the age of anxiety, afflicted with tunnel vision and distrust of our neighbors. The powerful influence of the hippie decades on American culture depended on the participation of a great number of people. It was a movement in the true sense of the word, a collective effort toward a common goal: personal freedom.

Now there are only separate movements in opposing directions and a seeming ambiguity of purpose. My generation has been characterized as thoughtless, cynical, unmotivated, apathetic and generally uninterested. Although I have known several people who fit the stereotype, I cannot blame them, but rather the circumstances of their experience. For many my age, our childhood took place just as our parents' euphoric awakening was drizzling into a confused haze of dissatisfaction. Families broke apart, divorce became common practice. During the past twenty years, technological innovation has become the dominant factor in defining the pace of our culture. Perhaps our brains seem a bit numb because they are saturated with too much information, too many media images repeating themselves in the reflective surfaces of our shiny new world. American culture thrives on appearances, swallows the grit and beauty that lies under its glassy facades and spits out the remains in dilapidated, dirty dollar signs. The disease of overconsumption is as familiar as the threat of being infected with HIV. Growing up amid all-you-can-eat buffets and Slim-Fast programs, we were taught early on to follow our appetites rather than our ideas.

As we move closer and closer to a new millennium, I am unsure of the space I occupy. I am compelled to walk away, backwards, away from the cars and blaring artificial lights, away from computer-generated greetings and complacent barstools, away from the mentality that caring about anything equates to naiveté. So here I am, driving through a landscape that has seen the last thirty years go whirling by in a blur of ever increasing traffic, rising decibels and thickening exhaust.

If we are moving in circles, they seem to be getting tinier and tinier. Maybe the equator is tightening its grasp on the earth. It's difficult to remember that we are just passing through, mere vessels complete with supple exteriors to accommodate the shifting states of our souls. When I turned twenty-three and moved to the country, I felt as if I could finally exhale that little bit of breath I'd been unconsciously holding in my lungs. Time is not so relentless when it is possible to watch the sun make an uninhibited arc across the day, when the stars take up more of the night's space than the darkness, when a footprint lives for days in its moist soil bed, when the only motor to be heard is the occasional tractor several miles away. I understand why my parents chose to spend this stage of their lives away from the commotion of urban America.

I am watching Iowa go by. This midwestern countryside is the place that possesses part of my childhood, the place where I caught snowflakes on my tongue and fireflies in Mason jars, imagining that I had captured things born of the stars. I don't know where I'm going, and even as I drive amid familiar territory, I wonder where I've been. Yet I have inherited a certain essence, a philosophy perhaps, from my parents, and it's not important for me to know. Possibility is a wind so strong it sometimes blows right through you. The same wind, perhaps, that carried the kite my parents and I flew recently on top of a big hill in Cedar County as the sun was setting one evening. That is where I will be—where I am—and all around me, Iowa is humming.

Diane B. Sigman

A Dual Life

diane b. sigman

I smoked my first joint three weeks before my eleventh birthday. With my mother. My mother had smoked her first roughly three years earlier, at age thirty-four. She got high with our neighbors, Michael and Caroline, who lived two houses down from us in suburban Detroit.

Prior to meeting Michael and Caroline, my middle-class parents listened to Johnny Mathis, wore polyester pants, ate Saturday night dinners at Joe Muir's Steakhouse, and socialized with other young Jewish couples who were beginning families and paying on starter homes. My father was a ham radio enthusiast; my mother played Mah-Jongg every Wednesday night with four other women. Bowel habits of the children dominated the conversation.

My brother's birth in 1971 made our starter home too small. My parents selected our new house from a tract going up quickly and cheaply over empty fields. All the houses were thin-walled and leaky. During winter months we put towels on the windowsills that stuck to ice in the screen tracks.

My mother met Caroline when our schnauzer, Margo, crapped on her expensive, chemically maintained lawn. My mother apologized—Margo had an annoying tendency to bolt when let out—and they fell to conversing. During the next few weeks, whenever I couldn't find my mother in the house, I'd stand on our driveway and look down the block. My mother would be sitting on Caroline's porch, the two of them chatting and smoking cigarettes bought by the carton.

Then Caroline introduced Michael to my mother, my father was brought in and my family experienced a sea change. I was seven, my sister, six, my brother, three. Born in 1967, I remember vast expanses of "before," including the Vietnam War, Watergate, my mother's bouffant hairdo and my father's leisure suit.

Michael and Caroline were thirteen years apart in age, smoked pot and listened to music we'd never heard before. Dionne Warwick, Eydie Gorme and Johnny Mathis records were soon shelved to make space for the Eagles and Fleetwood Mac. I came downstairs one morning and wandered over to the stereo, where an album lay out from the night before: *Led Zeppelin IV.* The gray man bent under his load of twigs looked a hell of a lot different from Dionne Warwick, insouciant in her Pucci sheath on the cover of *The Windows of the World.*

"Something is very different here," I remember thinking. "Something has changed."

Indeed. What Michael and Caroline offered my parents was a way station into something they were longing for but could not articulate. They were bored by those Joe Muir's dinners, talk of how many bags of grass clippings each garnered from the Saturday lawn mowing and whether or not the kids shat according to Spock. Michael and Caroline read books and listened to this weird music and talked about ideas. Michael liked to cook exotic foods. He belonged to a beer club and ordered aged steaks through the mail. Issues of *Gourmet* began turning up in our family room.

My mother stopped using lipstick and put her frosted blue eye shadow away. She stashed her hot rollers (whose smell while heating I loved) under the bathroom sink and threw away the CFC-laden can of Aqua Net. She began wearing flat shoes. My father abandoned his hair spray, grew a full beard and mustache and allowed his thick hair to grow in. Both began wearing jeans. They dropped their straight friends swiftly and without explanation.

Yet they did not become hippies. Detroit didn't produce hippies any more than it manufactured reliable cars. Instead, they became more open-minded, aware. They began to see societal mores as false constructs. Their relationship with Michael and Caroline deepened into an extended marriage.

Detroit wasn't a swinging L.A. or the remote hills of Humboldt County, where open marriages and casual attitudes toward drugs were more prevalent. The Detroit I grew up in was about White Flight and ostentatious money and moving to a house in West Bloomfield with a Cadillac—always a Cadillac—in the driveway. The mothers of my peers wore gold jewelry and tight designer jeans. Black women from the inner city cleaned these women's homes while they shopped and swapped divorce lawyers.

Although my parents never told me to be discreet, I intuited that ours was not a lifestyle discussed outside the house. I was in training for the dual life I maintain to this day. When I was younger, this meant getting a decent education and a job, limiting my drug exploits to weekends and keeping my counterculture views quiet among my peers. Neither of my parents had college degrees, and we thought that magic parchment meant financial security, infinitely more appealing than macaroni and old coats. So while I toked up with my folks on free Saturday nights, I also began accepting babysitting jobs whenever possible, spending those Friday and Saturday nights at somebody else's kitchen table, buried in American history or Spanish verb conjugation. Sometimes I'd get home around one or two in the morning, still silently conjugating the verb "to be" in Spanish, only to find my parents huddled around the table with Caroline and Michael, tapping Quaalude powder—still commercially available—into vitamin E capsules. Or they might be snorting a few lines. Pot was always around. I was frequently invited to join and just as often declined.

Sometime in my early teens, Caroline decided she didn't want to be married to Michael anymore. I have no idea why. I'm not sure anyone did. Michael moved to New Mexico to be with his son, Ian, the child of his brief first marriage. My parents were devastated, but continued their intense relationship with Caroline. Robert H. Rimmer's *The Harrad Experiment* and *Proposition 31* lay out in the family room. I read Rimmer's careful analyses of extended, loving relationships and felt they made perfect sense. A group of consenting adults wanting to share lives: sex, children, home, money. Yet I compared Rimmer's utopian world to my parents' lives: missing Michael, dependent on me for child care, low on cash and living in a house deteriorating under harsh midwestern winters. I resented the metal key chain that gave my neck a rash. Going off to live with a like-minded group of people who took care of each other sounded fine to me.

By high school I had my life down to a science. I attended classes in the morning, then worked in the high school's main office during the afternoon as part of the cooperative education program. I studied madly, enrolling in advanced placement history and English, hoping my good grades would get me loans or maybe a scholarship to Wayne State University. With my paychecks, I bought corduroy pants, matching sweaters and low-heeled boots. I kept my wavy brown hair shoulder-length and clean. Years later, reading *Jane Eyre*, I instantly identified with the protaganist's need to deflect attention from her person, keeping her shabby but neat clothing "in quaker trim."

My school job freed me from babysitting, so Saturday nights, my books neatly stacked in my dusted bedroom, I'd get high with my parents. My father had befriended some younger co-workers who were into cocaine. They'd come over with their girlfriends and assorted buddies and we'd party all night.

One buddy was a tall, shy young man named Dean. He came from a working-class Catholic family of nine brothers and sisters, many of whom worked alongside him at a Ford plant. Though he was sharply intelligent, college was never encouraged in his family.

So despite his desire to attend, he abided by his father's wishes and followed in the family footsteps into the safety of the United Auto Workers.

I fell madly in love with him. I was drawn to his quiet demeanor, the way he'd sit cross-legged on the floor at our parties, leaning forward occasionally to utter nearly inaudible comments. He liked to read, do drugs and ride motorcycles, and he turned me on to Neil Young. Our relationship encompassed all the clichés of passionate nights and dazed happiness. I was sixteen; Dean, twenty.

But we needed to score some birth control for those passionate nights. This was the early eighties, when the worst fears surrounding sexual contact could be cured with a script for penicillin. How innocently lucky we were, the last children of a halcyon era. Dean offered to buy condoms, but I felt wary: My sister was the product of a broken condom. I wanted the utter security of the Pill.

Even given their liberal views, the idea of hitting up my parents for birth control alarmed me. But one of our closest family friends, David, was an ob/gyn and my regular physician, so skulking off to the clinic my peers ducked into seemed ridiculous. While I screwed up the guts to ask my mom to make an appointment with David, Dean and I planned a trip to northern Michigan, where his family had a cabin.

My mother, of course, was no fool.

"So I guess you'll be needing some birth control," she said as we drove home from the supermarket a few weeks before the trip. I thought I was going to fall out of the Buick onto Southfield Road. "Uh, yeah, I will." Off we went to David's office, where he gave me six months of Ortho-Novum and the freedom to fuck unfettered.

Driving back, my mother told me never to have sex in cars, as Detroit at night is not only dangerous, but often chilly. "Go in your bedroom and put the stereo on for privacy," she suggested. "That way, I won't have to worry about where you are. And you won't catch cold."

Dean and I were together for just under a year. Initially we were happy, but our differences surfaced quickly. His family was openly anti-Semitic and they made their dislike of me plain. I didn't allow the rush of sex and late nights of coke-fueled talk to interrupt my studies. Dean, who did differential equations on grocery lists when bored, was openly jealous. I pushed him hard to borrow money and attend a local technical college. It was none of my business, and he told me so. In truth, the college argument was indicative of deeper, irreconcilable differences. Dean came from a family that attended church on Sundays, sought other churchgoing, blue-collar people to marry and continued the tradition of large families. What I naively saw as somebody longing for more, as my parents had years earlier, was simply a boy having his wild youth before settling down to a nice housewife who would dutifully produce babies and obey the man of the house.

And then there was the cocaine. Lots of it. More than I'd ever seen. One of his brothers was a dealer, so we paid little for pure eight balls—an eighth of an ounce—folded into intricate paper squares cut from *Playboy*. Dean and two of his brothers were addicted. Lines in the morning before work, lines in the bathroom, lines in the car off a hand mirror while driving. (I never understood the mechanics of that maneuver. And didn't other drivers, specifically the police, ever notice?) While I liked cocaine, my gaze never wavered from my savior from poverty: a college education. The drug waited in my night-table drawer, tucked into my blue leather "concert kit" until Friday night. "How can you have it in the house and not do it?" Dean would ask. "When I have it, I do it until it's gone."

His friends were equally amazed. I remember hanging out at the house he shared with his brothers one Wednesday night. The usual crowd was drifting around, waiting for free lines. Coke dealers always have lots of friends. Dean's brother Trey, the dealer, arranged four neat lines on the Miller High Life mirror and shoved them across the table to where I sprawled on the couch. "Hey everybody! Watch this! Watch her not do it!" The four lines sat between us, untouched, until some impatient soul reached down with a rolled bill and got high on a school night.

Our relationship ended acrimoniously. For Christmas I bought Dean a watch he'd been eyeing for months. He promptly "lost" it. Whether he truly did, sold it for drugs or broke it in anger after a fight with me I cannot say. He ruefully promised to replace it "as soon as he had the money." I watched him put four or five watches up his nose before realizing cocaine meant more to him than the thirty-seven dollars I'd painfully saved from my meager school job. We broke up in an ugly, sobbing scene on New Year's Eve, and I have not seen him since.

The breakup devastated me. I missed him so much it felt physical. I imagined him finding a skinny, narrow-hipped Catholic girl—at size twelve, I was too voluptuous for his tastes—and marrying her. Having quiet, nearsighted babies and buying his starter home on Detroit's east side, far from the reviled Jews and Blacks. I still think about him and wonder if he's tamped down our relationship into something meaningless, or if he looks at his wife in the night and wonders what he missed.

A few other people wandered in and out of my family's lives. Ian, Michael's son, was an occasional visitor, always bringing drugs, a bag of new records and an enviably sexy girlfriend. He went in for tall, collected redheads or blondes who left me quailing, so positive in my stoned stupor that I would say something stupid, I'd lapse into paranoid silence.

There were others: William, who discussed the scientific versus the aesthetic structure of the world with me on a long walk one day when I was seven; a guy Ian often crashed with named Blaster; and Cecilia, who'd been gang-raped at a party while tripping on LSD. Talented, bright, charismatic, they'd arrive unexpectedly from Lansing or Grand Rapids or Kalamazoo, illuminating the house for a few hours with laughter and talk, then disappearing just as quickly, returning in six days or four months or never again. These people were either incapable of or uninterested in ongoing friendships. It seemed to me that the more people "understood things," the less capable they were of functioning in the world, barely getting by on parental dole or dealing. William's brilliance turned the corner to insanity; last I heard he lived in the streets. Blaster moved from place to place, dealing. Cecilia married a straight, dull fellow and had babies. Ian did nothing, dropping out of college and living off Michael, collecting a string of pretty girls who eventually tired of his laziness and dumped him. My combination of good student, outstanding co-op worker of the year, and drug-user with my folks on weekends, while odd, wasn't impossible. Why didn't other people do it?

During my teens, I remember surveying our lives, relative to the world around us. The straight route led to financial freedom, affording me the creature comforts I wanted: books, records and nice clothing. The counterculture neglected the material things, shunning those values as "square," offering instead people who shared some of my core values about politics and drugs, people who didn't freak out over my parents. A foot in both worlds struck me as practical and not a particularly difficult way to live. I often hid my glee in high school, the model student in the front row as the counselors raved at us about the dangers of drugs.

I spent countless hours trying to figure out people like Ian, who did absolutely nothing, or Cecilia, who crossed into the straight life with nary a backward glance. Ultimately I gave up, becoming wary and distant from the parade through our home. Attachment to these people, however appealing, only meant hurt when they vanished. And, invariably, they did.

Friendless and unspeakably lonely, I despaired of finding people who shared my world view. My peers were a bunch of smart, rich kids following the party line, wearing Levi's with the waist size blacked out, meeting their future spouses at B'nai B'rith youth group meetings, readying their applications to the University of Michigan. Their predictable behavior patterns enraged me. I had no desire to be like them. I wanted them to be like me.

When I was seventeen, my family decided to move to Los Angeles, where my father could find lucrative employment in the burgeoning defense industry. I was thrilled to leave, thinking of California's then-affordable state colleges and of all the hip, like-thinking people I'd befriend or date. Only my mother cried when we left Caroline behind.

My father found a job at a big defense company doing government contract work. He loathed it and everything it represented, but we had medical insurance, were able to replace the rusted-out station wagon and could even afford to go see Tom Petty at the Universal Amphitheater. A local kid sold us something we'd never heard of, "skunk," pot so powerful it left my sister giggling helplessly in the bathtub.

The move gave us an enormous culture shock. People spoke unrecognizable valley-girl English. Strip malls lined every non-residential street, each anchored by a nail salon. People were enthralled by their fingernails and their weight. The weather was the same every day: hot, dry and unbearably bright. Our first Christmas in L.A. utterly unnerved me. I had taken a terrible job with an insurance company while waiting to establish residency for college. The city had overdecorated, as if compensating for the eighty-five degree heat. I remember emerging from the office building at noon, Christmas Eve, hitting that blast of dry Santa Ana heat and wanting to kill myself.

My depression deepened into a constant that varied only in intensity. I remember finishing Simone de Beauvoir's *The Mandarins* during my sophomore year. It was the final day before the month-long holiday break, and the campus was deserted, smelling (finally) of winter and dry leaves. An empty month lay ahead. Even the book, with its fascinating characters who led full, exciting lives, was finished. I dropped it reluctantly in the library return slot and thought again about suicide.

At twenty-two I had a nervous breakdown. I was doing well in school, but it wasn't enough to pull me up from the emptiness of my personal life. I ceased functioning at home, crying constantly and sleeping as much as possible. I became obsessed with my weight and the most efficient way to commit suicide.

Fortunately, I was still living with my parents. My sister had moved in with a boyfriend. My brother, who was fourteen when we arrived, had made the best adjustment, getting his GED, a good job and a nice car in short order. He was busy playing in bands and going out to Hollywood clubs with his many friends. So my parents, who weren't meeting scads of people themselves, had plenty of time to babysit me. For the next two years, I lived in a bizarre netherworld, finishing my B.A. and falling apart. For a while I was incapable of going to the supermarket alone. I'd stand there, bewildered: What did we need? Why was I there? If I stayed in my bedroom with the stereo on for more than a half hour, my mother pounded on the door until I came out. She walked dozens of miles with me around our subdivision as I ranted about ending my life.

I visited a therapist in a tony office on Ventura Boulevard. The color of her suit matched her shoes and fingernails. She told me I was an intellectual snob and needed to go Jewish folk danc-ing, where I would meet nice boys. "Call me," she offered while ushering me out, "if you feel suicidal over the weekend." "You," I thought, "are the last person I'd call."

Eventually the worst of it lifted. I graduated with honors. My brother moved out to pursue his nocturnal music career. I remained in our large house. I paid my parents a little rent and continued to help around the house.

At twenty-five I met my husband through a personals ad I placed in an alternative newspaper. I was meeting no men, the ad was free, I had nothing to lose. I received hundreds of responses, finally hitting on the line "looks and money not important" to win-now out callers boasting of "industry" jobs, yachts and horse ranches. John's voice message only said: "Call me and we'll savage the right."

We met for coffee and nursed cappuccinos for three hours. We met at Venice Beach and strolled the boardwalk, poking into bookstores and head shops. I told my mother, "We get along."

"You're going to marry him," she said.

It would be disingenuous to close with counterculture girl met counterculture boy, had counterculture wedding (the groom wore shoulder-length hair and a Jerry Garcia tie; the bride didn't have a manicure) and lived happily ever after. We each continue to act in two worlds. John is an environmental engineer with an international company that drug tests its employees. His gorgeous long hair rests in an envelope in his desk drawer.

John has a rare chromosomal aberration called Becker Muscular Dystrophy. It is a slow wasting of the leg and hip muscles, sometimes compounded by pulmonary and cardiac complications. Recent medical research has prolonged the lives of those afflicted, but we live with the knowledge that we may not grow old together.

He was diagnosed at sixteen and promptly decided to live

as he wished and fight like hell. His attitude gives mine ballast. Unlike me, John had many friends when we met, some close. I had long before internalized the idea that the only relationships worth pursuing were of the Caroline and Michael variety. I learned from John that an acquaintance based on a few shared interests can be rewarding, and that such relationships don't represent the surrender of core values. Instead, they are companionship, a shared glass of wine or a hit, a pleasant evening, a party to attend. I learned not to expect an intense communion at every encounter.

In fact, I stopped looking for it. I now have a few friends. None are remotely like the relationships I witnessed growing up. I am still lonely, though less so, and prone to bouts of depression. I suspect I always shall be. But knowing my happy marriage may not last forces me to attend to the present.

I am now thirty-one years old and hold to my early pursuit of a foot in each world. To an extent, I feel alienated by each; I'd no sooner vote for Elizabeth Dole than I'd live without running water. This lands me in a gray place, going into the straight world for my paycheck, then veering toward the counterculture for a reaffirmation of my values.

My parents, now in their late fifties, continue their countercultural ways, fond as ever of lava lamps and always the oldest attendees at rock concerts. After an earthquake damaged their home, they moved to the Southwest, to a blindingly bright white house that deflects the desert sun. Surrounding them are young Mormon couples who make their anti-Semitism plain. Membership in the homeowners' association is mandatory.

So my parents move quietly, pulling the drapes before

switching on the lava lamps, keeping bottles of air freshener on the coffee table in case a neighbor knocks. They have made a few acquaintances, all younger. They do not know where Michael and Caroline are; at times, my mother insists they are dead.

For all intents and purposes, they are. But a breeze continues to blow through the window that they opened.

River Light

Ghosts

river light

Thirty-one years ago a baby girl slipped into this world. Spoon-fed love and wild ways, she grew to be a rag-tag tangle-haired woods baby. Small child thriving on the seeds of rebellious plants, rebellious ideas. Child encircled in the arms of a culture running counter to concrete streets, camouflaged intent and white bread, white sugar ideas.

Who I am is informed by, but not defined by, the fact that I am a "hippie kid." I stand in too many camps for only two feet, and the camps are not always at peace. I am an avid feminist and an anti-censorship, pro-sex "pervert." I believe in decadence, but cannot become passionate about money. I am a dyke who wants children, a woods baby living in the heart of the city, a pacifist who has taken self-defense.

We were the golden children, angels of the woods.

My stepmother (long since left my dad) worries that I do not prepare for my retirement, while my father (still the hippie radical dropout) worries that I do not prepare for the fall. My mother, burned by "free love," worries that I'll be stung by the polyamory that I embrace, and my stepfather keeps his own counsel.

The child whose first word was "hot," but whose second was . . . possibly not fit for the company of grandparents. A child who understood the concepts but who, stretching at the applications, still asked, "Is this one of those times I don't say 'fuck'?" The child who ate with four forks, three knives, some spoons, but mainly her hands. Who now reads entire books on manners (the last one titled, appropriately enough, Please Don't Eat the Doily). *The one who now prides herself in knowing how to formally introduce.*

I come from two "failed marriages." But with each separation and subsequent addition, those who cherish me grew in number. And my love for my original parents did not diminish. I had ample for all—and so do not believe in the scarcity theory of love. I do not believe affection is finite, because that has never been my experience.

The child who would climb into anyone's lap, even if only just introduced, because a friend is a friend regardless of how long the acquaintance.

Nothing lasts forever. Each friendship, each relationship, must change, flow through its cycles, transform endlessly into new gifts, new treasures. If we resist this movement, the relationship shatters, like ice in the moving tide. But if we are open to re-creation, then we become stronger with each new turn.

Child brought up on Gandhi. Who presumed good intent, and love as the common denominator. Child taught to move gently through this good life—that each action, no matter how small, affects the whole.

I can no more write of the deadening pain of loss than I can of the breathless confusion of new love. Love's ecstasy is like being stoned on almost too many mushrooms: Those who've never tried it have no comparison; those who have still do not share a common experience. Each trip takes you down a different path. And to paint a picture of true loss is to create something that is indecipherable to the uninitiated and unbearable to those who have felt its paralysis deaden the senses.

The child who, for all her strengths, all her freedoms, is nevertheless but a child. Still must be fed, must be cared for, must be raised, by others. Cannot choose to remain behind as life's sudden changes take those who love her elsewhere.

When I was ten years old I lost my home. I left the wilderness completely and began to live full time in the city. Twenty-one years later I still define my life history in terms of before and after. How does a child mourn this loss? My home was not broken, it was abandoned in a process that started at age four when my parents separated, and my brother and I began to live half-time with my mother in the city. It was completed six years later, when my father, left abruptly by my stepmother, could no longer care for my brother and me adequately one month out of every two.

The child who at age eleven is shocked to discover that people, that a friend, can look one in the eye and lie. Who sits on the steps of the first real school she has ever attended, and weeps at her disillusionment, at the seeming uncertainty of everything, at the changing laws of the universe.

Home is where my family is. When my mom comes in to wish me goodnight and ends up curled next to me, talking over the latest in our lives—I am home. When my father and I work shoulder to shoulder preparing the fire pit circle for guests—I am home. When my stepmom opens the door of her new house to me, one that I have never before visited—I am home. When my brother's children climb into my lap—I am home. When I lie in my bed, my lover's head on my chest, our skin damp from lovemaking—I am home.

And yet there is a child who can never go home. A little girl who knew a home that worked its way into each cell, that grew to become the strength of her bones, a part of her skin—integral to the workings of her lungs, her heart. A home that smells of rain and of sunshine on salty rocks. A home that sounds like silence, but which is as silent as a tidepool is empty. A home that tastes like the first salmonberries of spring, fresh-picked huckleberries, dried saskatoon berries too late in

*the season. A home that feels like the earth under bare feet, the cool
woods air on naked skin, the salal scraping your thighs as you push
your way through it. A child who, yearning to go back, must learn to
turn and face forward.*

I dream of holding my own children to my breast. Of leaning back
into the arms of my partners, my lovers, and feeling their lives en-
twined with mine as far into the future as I can see. So often the
memory of loss, the pain of past loves' endings, clouds my vision
and I turn from my dreams, frightened by the innocence, the intensity, of my hope.

But I *will* stand, one day, at my own hearth. A hearth encircled by
the people of my present, of my future. A hearth not haunted by
ghosts.

Rivka K. Solomon

Thanksgiving '71

rivka k. solomon

1971 was the year my sandwiches went from Wonderbread to whole wheat with wheatberries. From velvet dissolving in my mouth to gritty cardboard that needed to be chewed forever.

In '71, no one in my elementary school was eating PB & J on brown bread. Between bites I hid my sandwich under the lunchroom table.

In '71, my family moved in with strangers—people who grew pot on the windowsills, shared hot oil massages in the living room and danced around the kitchen to reggae while boiling lentils.

In '71 we shunned supermarkets. We bought groceries from the Unitarian Church weekly food co-op—even all-natural turkey and organic brown rice stuffing.

✦

"Do I haaave to?" I whined more now that I lived with strangers and ate brown food.

"Don't you want to pay respect to Mother Earth? Do something symbolic with soil on this sacred day?" Mom asked.

She was serious.

I was nine.

I shrugged and put my mittens on.

It was dusk and so cold you could see your breath. We stood over the frostbitten tomato plants in the garden. Mom read poetry by Native Americans. Dad tried to get a shovel into the frozen compost. (Something symbolic.) Each adult said why she was thankful. My sister rolled her eyes and stomped her feet to keep warm.

"Didn't Pilgrims kill Indians?" I whispered to her.

"Yeah, Pilgrims were jerks," she whispered back. She was eleven, knew more and was much cooler than I.

"Why do we celebrate Thanksgiving if Pilgrims were jerks?" I asked. All the adults looked at me.

"I can't feel my face," my sister said. "I'm going inside."

We all followed, except Dad, determined to get his shovelful.

The mashed potatoes had brown worms mixed in. Or maybe they were just the skins.

"Most nutritious part," Mom said.

"High in vitamin A," said Dad.

"I think it's D," she corrected.

Somebody lit a joint.

I poked a drumstick with my fork. I'd seen a turkey farm on TV that morning. So many birds, all dead now. I thought about becoming the youngest vegetarian in America.

"Eat your salad," Dad said.

It was covered with tofu-tamari dressing. Brown liquid with white clumps, clinging to green leaves. I shook my head no.

"Why not?" he asked.

I bit into the cranberry sauce. My face puckered. Saliva rushed to my mouth.

"Sugar's bad for you," a man from the commune said when I spit it out.

"I know," I retorted and grabbed some pie to save my palate: bland and thick with pumpkin strings.

"I made that too," he said.

Dishes piled, oil heating on the stove, the adults retreated to the living room.

"Oops, nature calls," a woman of the commune said. She rose

from the pillows, skipped past the bathroom and out the rear door into the wooded backyard.

I was so glad I hadn't invited any friends over that year.

The next school day at lunchtime I peeked under the table into my sandwich baggie.

Dead bird.

My stomach growled, but I still couldn't do it.

In 1971, the youngest vegetarian in America decided brown bread with just ketchup wasn't so bad.

Suzanne M. Cody

Rewriting History

suzanne m. cody

*D*ear Isabel, aged four and a half months:

It is 8:30 P.M. It's November. It snowed today. Not a lot, just a little, enough that you noticed it touching your fat little hands and chubby pink cheeks when I carried you out on the porch to see it. There was a sharp breeze from off the harbor and you started making that breathless "Huh-huh-huh" sound like the wind was whipping your little baby breath right out of your lungs. I brought you inside right away because I don't think that sound indicates pleasure or delight. I could be wrong. I'm still pretty new at this baby thing.

It is 8:30 P.M. and you are asleep and I should be, but I am up looking at my reflection in the kitchen window, eating generic Applejacks with rice milk and wondering at the fact that I am lucky enough to be your mother. I have never been lucky. It has to be a fluke. You are so lovely and alive and aware and I am clearly too unbalanced and insecure to be your mother—to be anybody's mother. But then I love you so intensely and I find myself consistently doing my best to do the right things for you. And for the kitty, too, who is currently constipated and leaving little shit trails on the kitchen linoleum where he drags his impacted butt. You and the kitty both have poop problems and need glycerin suppositories. This is so much of my life now, your poop, the kitty's poop—I have become a mother. A challenged mother, but a mother just the same. And I am constantly blown away by that one fact. *I am a mother.*

This afternoon you were cranky—your teeth are coming in early and painfully like your mama's before you and I deeply need to understand why childhood has to hurt so much. Design flaws? Or is this supposed to build infant character? I strapped your small fussy self to my chest, twisting and folding the Maine Baby Bag so you could look outward without a strap cutting across your face. I think it's designed to work like that. Still, I kept walking into the bathroom to check in the mirror and make sure your lips weren't turning blue. That would be just like me—accidentally killing you when I am just trying to make you feel better. But you fell asleep dangling off me like an extra appendage and I stood at the kitchen counter thinking and rocking. (Stand several young mothers together in a group and in moments they will all be rocking back and forth at just about heartbeat speed. Not only will they not notice themselves, they won't notice anyone else doing it either.)

Ani DiFranco is spouting Riot Grrl dogma from a cheap boom box I bought at a pawnshop. Our welfare checks won't even cover the rent. I just smashed my glasses all to hell rolling around on the floor with you. The phone bill is seventy-five dollars and that's mostly service charges. I am paying off a defaulted student loan. The hospital is hounding me for the rest of the cost of your birth—I would think labor would be payment enough, for christ's sake. But you would still be worth every penny, if I had it, if we had it. Someone once told me it was better to have no money because then you didn't have to worry about what you were going to do with it. Clearly, that person had money and no children.

What you and I look like isn't quite the picture I had in my head when I envisioned having a baby, my only baby. I didn't see a secondhand crib and store-brand disposable diapers. I didn't see innumerable calls to the Department of Human Services and long mornings trying to make you be patient in government waiting rooms. I didn't see a low-income housing apartment full of furniture scavenged from the unburned sheds on Nonny and Grampa's property. No. No, this isn't quite it. But it's okay—it's okay. I have you, and creative poverty is a familiar coat to wear, and we have it pretty good, considering.

I am going to make sure that you understand that these aren't the things that count, in the end, in the big picture. I try to keep that in perspective. We live like this so I can be home for you, with you, to make sure, absolutely sure that you do have the *really* important things. When you cry, I am the one who picks you up right away. When you are hungry, you have the comfort of my breast. When you are tired, I am the one who rocks you to sleep. I know the games and the blanket and the toy you like. I have witnessed every developmental breakthrough and have cheered you on. I want you to feel safe and stable and secure in the knowledge that I am here for you, and that I will always be here for you and it doesn't matter how our life looks from the outside. Here, on the inside, things are as they should be. You can depend on me, okay? Okay.

Unsolicited advice is the mainstay of motherhood, and generally the bane of single motherhood. If you make an unpopular parenting decision (like, oh, exclusively breastfeeding the baby for six months—or, even worse, *co-sleeping*), you have no one to support you, to back you up. No one to consult, to ask "What do you think about . . . ?" I have a deep and desperate need for you to have an interesting, creative, healthy childhood. Not having a basis for comparison or anyone I'd particularly trust to give me advice on that topic—the healthy part, anyway—I'm sort of winging it. Taking that into consideration, what do you say we lay down a couple of ground rules, just between the two of us, and talk about them later, eventually, when you figure out how to express yourself in words. This mother/baby thing is pretty fluid, but it would be nice to have a few things to be sure of. Okay? Okay.

I, Isabel's mama, do solemnly swear (in no particular order):

. . . not to leave pot brownies where you might get into them.

. . . not to ever send you blithely off to school dressed like an extra from *Hair*. It was a Cody family outing when the movie came to town, and yes, I went to school the next day in a long flowing skirt, a gauzy blouse and flowers in my hair.

. . . to have a car that runs reliably and has heat, a complete floor and no "creative paint job." My most memorable childhood ride consisted of a partially burnt out, candy-apple red Volkswagen bus replete with painted underwater views on both sides and "The

Nautilus" in curlicue script on the doors. Right here would be a good place to let you know that I was never, as a child, ashamed of your grandparents or our groovy hipster life out in the middle of nowhere. (We lived in Freedom, of all places, in the immediate vicinity of Unity and Liberty.) Granted, the people we were surrounded by were similar—young couples and families escaping back to the land from various major metropolitan areas, a lot of artists and writers and performers. Most are divorced now, and many of their kids are lazy or crazy or both. Go figure. But the *point*, my angel, is I never thought twice about being chauffeured around in that bohemian behemoth. In fact, I was likely pretty pleased with it at the time. Yet, one blindingly rainy, windy, miserable New England afternoon as your Uncle Nik, Aunt Gwennie and I bounced around, unseatbelted and carseatless in the cavernous rear of The Nautilus, your Nonny was struggling to control the car against the weather. Dwarfed at four feet ten and one hundred pounds by the entire counterculture driving experience, Nonny peered anxiously ahead for oncoming lights as the bus wove back and forth across the double yellow line. She didn't see any, but the more minuscule rear guard paused from its raucous game among groceries and clean laundry to note the flashing blues coming up behind. "I smell bacon!" we shouted as Nonny hauled the bus to the side of the road.

So, up walked Mr. Backwoods Cop, thinking, certainly, that he was about to make a major drug bust—buncha fucked-up hippies can't even control their psy-che-del-ic-ve-hi-cle—and what did he find? One harried little woman and three slightly grungy children. There was a short pause as he stood outside Nonny's window, rain pouring off the brim of his hat. Then he told her to be more cautious driving in heavy weather and walked back to his car, clearly disappointed to have nothing of substance to tell the boys at the diner. Of course, had he looked, he might have found a little something in the ashtray.

. . . to always have enough money for food. Our short, moneyless phase was difficult enough when I was a proud little kid. How many times did your Nonny try to hand me food stamps as I headed out the door with the other kids to buy chips and Cokes at the general store? And how many times would I spend my money instead, money from babysitting or collecting bottles by the roadside, and do without non-food things I could have spent it on instead?

. . . to use wood heat only in a decorative holiday fireplace or as an emergency backup to the thermostat.

. . . that sleeping in tents will be for recreational purposes only and certainly never a necessity *in* the house. When my family first moved from the one-room hunting camp that was our temporary Freedom residence to the one-room cabin that became our permanent one, we had to sleep in tents pitched in second-floor lofts, tucked under the peaked roof. The walls were so full of holes that without the tents we would have been nothing but mosquito meat. The cabin did tighten and expand, eventually, into an actual house. Your grandfather had a penchant for taking his chainsaw to walls, ceilings and floors whenever that expansion mood took him.

It's all gone now. The house we built from logs hauled from the woods and fields on our property burned to the ground last year during those crazy ice storms—two and a half months after I found out I was pregnant with you, one month after Nonny finally got fed up with Grampa's drinking and left, two weeks after your Uncle Nik and your Grampa held a wild holiday bash that completely trashed the house. *C'est la vie.*

. . . to give you limits and guidelines, and discipline you when you willfully and unreasonably defy me.

. . . to sometimes disapprove of your clothes, your habits, your friends, your music. I had to make an intense and creative effort to rebel against Nonny and Grampa. What's left when your parents are giving you your dope, when you talk to your mom in detail about your sex life, when your dad likes to listen to louder music than you do, when you can come and go pretty much as you please? Or when you want to dress like Annie Hall and your mom thinks you should dress like Janis Joplin? Or when your parents think your rebel boyfriend who drinks too much, listens to punk rock music, lives on his skateboard and is constantly getting suspended from school is a really cool guy? Where do you go from there? Either you become a drug addict or a Republican. Or both.

. . . not to have you pass out free puppies or political bumperstickers at country fairs.

. . . to let you be a child for your entire childhood. When I turned eleven, your grandpa told me I could leave home whenever I wanted—eleven was old enough to take care of myself. Or, if I wasn't going to leave, I could at least participate in the family as a fully functioning adult. When Grampa had his first free-love affair that we knew about, he and Nonny talked about it with me—and I was about twelve. I put Nonny and your aunt and uncle upstairs in Nonny's bedroom to watch TV and sat downstairs alone, waiting for Grampa to come home from a self-abusive drunken tear to have it out with him myself.

Drugs were also a big issue between your grandparents and me right around this time. Once they didn't make it home until dawn because they accidentally took Quaaludes thinking they were speed and fell asleep on someone's couch. "Never," I scolded, "take anything unless you are *absolutely sure* of what it is." I think kids these days take for granted how little responsibility they have— the nineties are much more restrictive about parental sex and drug usage. But getting parents to use condoms might be more than even I am ready to deal with.

. . . to have indoor plumbing.

. . . that you will always feel safe around the people I bring into our lives—and if you don't, that you will feel able to tell me. One of Nonny and Grampa's friends in particular made me distinctly nervous. If he dropped by when I was alone, he would stick around for a while to chat. Nothing ever happened, but I do remember standing at the kitchen sink one afternoon taking a very long time to wash a carving knife as he lingered and asked me questions about my boyfriends—who they were, what I did with them. I was eleven and hadn't really gotten around to boyfriends yet (though it wouldn't be long). I just kept washing that knife over and over, rubbing the sponge along the blade as if I were meticulously removing every possible invisible particle of food. One clean knife.

. . . that there will be no part of my life that you are privy to that you can't talk about at school—you'll know what I mean one day. Or maybe you won't, since I haven't indulged on a regular basis since I was twenty and don't see that changing any time soon.

I'll warn you now, though, that under the influence of marijuana the women in our family miss out on the good stuff and pass out immediately. If we use it at all, it's for insomnia and menstrual cramps. Also, I will not be your teacher or your dealer. I knew how to roll a joint when I was twelve—Grampa taught me. And I have never in my life bought a bag of weed.

...to teach you to dance like Nonny taught me. We are great dancers—loose hips, don't you know.

...to teach you independence while still letting you depend on me.

...not to subject you to views of my male friends' penises. I had a pretty good idea what constituted big and small in the penile arena before I was ten. The swimming hole was bathing-suit optional, or more like bathing-suit discouraged—at least until the kids (namely me, as the oldest) reached puberty at which point nudity became divided along the age line.

...to always surround you with energy and creativity. Notwithstanding a little of this, a little of that, I want so much for your childhood to resemble the best parts of mine. Sneaking out my bedroom window and down the woodshed roof to skinny-dip with the boys on sticky summer nights. Coming home from school to *General Hospital* (the groovy Luke and Laura Ice Palace years) and hot tea and fresh bread on blue-cold winter afternoons. Dressing up in costume and walking in innumerable parades, leading kazoo bands, singing at parties, performing in variety shows, acting in plays. Learning how to cane chairs and grow sweet peas, can tomatoes and freeze spinach, make macramé necklaces, forge chain mail, ride a unicycle, juggle pins, putty windows, chink walls, spud logs, paddle a canoe, sail a catamaran. Contra-dancing. Scavenging for lunch in gardens. Knowing what a fresh vegetable tastes like. Picking wild strawberries and raspberries and blackberries. Helping animals into the world. Stretching out in a field on a cool autumn night, someone's thigh for your pillow, your stomach someone else's, watching the stars and humming Beatles songs.

. . . to teach you to *trust* people and to love them with all your heart and soul. Okay, I admit you'll get hurt. A lot. But it's worth it, I promise. I promise. I promise.

. . . to be a good mother to you, whatever that means. Whatever you need that to mean.

We will talk. When you can talk.

All my love,

Mama

Contributors

Paola Bilbrough is a New Zealand poet and reviewer based in Melbourne, Australia. Her collection of poems, *Bell Tongue,* was published in June 1999 by Victoria University Press in New Zealand. She is currently working on a novel. From time to time she still thinks nostalgically of communal, subsistence living.

Carin Clevidence attended Oberlin College and the University of Michigan and received a Fellowship at the Fine Arts Work Center in Provincetown, Massachusetts. Her work has appeared in *Story, Field, Grand Tour* and the *Asahi Weekly* of Japan. She lives on the south shore of Long Island with her husband and daughter and is currently at work on a novel.

Suzanne M. Cody and her daughter Isabel are currently residing in Iowa City, Iowa, with Isabel's father. Suzanne divides her time between being Mama and working at Prairie Lights Books while looking for the next writing project worth giving up nap time for.

Zoë Eakle was born and raised off the West Coast of Canada in British Columbia. She currently resides in Vancouver where she is an actor, writer and member of the performance group Taste This. She writes largely for performance but has recently made the leap to the printed page with the 1998 release of *Boys Like Her: Transfictions*, a book of short stories from performance written with fellow Taste This members and released by Press Gang Publishers in Vancouver.

Ariel Gore is the editor of *hip mama, the parenting zine* (www.hipmama.com), and the author of *The Hip Mama Survival Guide* (Hyperion, 1998).

Rain Grimes is an aspiring photographer and currently works as a photography assistant. She graduated from the University of Washington with a degree in literature and has worked at several independent publishing companies and as a production assistant for television commercials. She is inspired by music and poetry and images, and hopes to one day find or create a career that incorporates all three. She lives in Seattle.

Angela Lam lives a double life. By day, she roams the streets of Northern California selling real estate, armed with a pager and voice mail. By night, she haunts the bookstores and cafes giving poetry and prose readings with the shadow of her son in the wings. She took time off in 1997 to attend a writer's retreat at Hedgebrook in Washington State where she was able to indulge fully in a pampered bohemian lifestyle. She doesn't think her two identities will ever merge; some people still know her by two different names.

River Light is a thirty-one-year-old writer, actor, feminist, dyke and videomaker (among other things). She has a B.A. in Fine and Performing Arts from Simon Fraser University. River's essays and erotic stories have been published in a variety of places. In 1998 she co-facilitated a panel/workshop titled "Writing Porn" for Write Out West, a gay/lesbian/bisexual/transgendered writers conference. Light's work in video has been shown on Rogers Cablevision and on Coast 11 Cablevision, and a two-minute video she created won first prize in the audio/video category of the UN pavilion's Messages Of Peace contest at Expo86. Her play, *A Thin Line*, has been produced twice and was chosen for the juried performance festival Vancouver Women in View.

Lisa Michaels is the author of *Split: A Counterculture Childhood* and a contributing editor at the *Threepenny Review*. Her work has appeared in *Glamour, Salon* and the *New York Times Magazine*.

Cecily Schmidt is currently traveling the country with the man she loves, not searching for anything in particular, yet finding so much, trying to learn what it means to have acquired a Bachelor of Fine Arts degree from the University of Iowa, cherishing clean water, drawing pictures and collecting words, staying in constant motion, checking out art therapy graduate programs and possible places to live when the time comes to be stationary again.

Elizabeth Shé is the author of the novel *Shoulds Are for Saints: The True Life Adventures of Suzy Le Speed.* Her work has appeared in the 2 girls press anthology, *Northwest Edge: New Writings from the Pacific Northwest.* She is the former editor and publisher of *MEOW,* a Seattle arts journal.

Diane B. Sigman lives in Northern California. She wishes to express her profound love and gratitude to her husband, John, and to her parents, who generously permitted her to share their story.

Rivka K. Solomon continues to steer clear of turkey ("Pass the tofu, please"). She is currently writing a memoir about growing up as the daughter of some of Boston's earliest feminist activists. She is also editing a book of short narratives by gutsy females, *That Takes Ovaries! Bold Females and Their Brazen Acts.*

Chelsea Cain spent her early childhood eating organic tomatoes off the vine on a commune in Iowa. The magic and hope of her girlhood continue to shape her. But she still hates carob. The author of *Dharma Girl: A Road Trip Across the American Generations* (Seal, 1996), she works as a freelance writer and lives in Portland, Oregon.

Photo credits

All photos not otherwise credited are courtesy of the author.

Paola Bilbrough, page 179 by Kanako Hiramoto; Chelsea Cain, page 103 by Mary Cain, page 189 by Jason Hughes; Carin Clevidence, page 63 by Jennifer Clements, page 180 by Tim Fisher; Zoë Eakle, page 181 by Marianna Neuman; Ariel Gore, page 181 by Kathy Sloane; Rain Grimes, page 91 by Kristeen Griffin-Grimes, page 182 by Rain Grimes; Cecily Schmidt, page 184 by Chelsea Cain; Elizabeth Shé, page 185 by Eric Ramsey; Diane B. Sigman, page 186 by Stephanie L. Jackson; Rivka K. Solomon, page 186 by Bobbi Ausubel.

Selected Titles from Seal Press

For more than thirty years, Seal Press has published groundbreaking books. By women. For women. Visit our website at www.sealpress.com.

Waking Up American: Coming of Age Biculturally edited by Angela Jane Fountas. $15.95, 1-58005-136-7. Twenty-two original essays by first-generation women caught between two worlds. Countries of origin include the Philippines, Germany, India, Mexico, China, Iran, Nicaragua, Japan, Russia, and Panama.

The F-Word: Feminism in Jeopardy by Kristin Rowe-Finkbeiner. $14.95, 1-58005-114-6. An astonishing look at the tenuous state of women's rights and issues in America, and a call to action for the young women who have the power to change their situation

Cunt:A Declaration of Independence by Inga Muscio. $14.95, 1-58005-075-1. An ancient title of respect, "cunt" long ago veered off the path of honor and now careens toward the heart of every woman as expletive. Muscio traces this winding road, giving women both the motivation and the tools to claim "cunt" as a positive and powerful force in the lives of women.

Solo: On Her Own Adventure edited by Susan Fox Rogers. $14.95, 1-58005-137-5. An inspiring collection of travel narratives that reveal the complexities of women journeying alone.

Listen Up: Voices from the Next Feminist Generation edited by Barbara Findlen. $16.95, 1-58005-054-9. A collection of eight essays featuring the voices of today's young feminists on racism, sexuality, identity, AIDS, revolution, abortion and much more.

Body Outlaws: Rewriting the Rule of Beauty and Body Image edited by Ophira edut, foreward by Rebecca Walker. $15.95, 1-58005-108-1. In a culture where plastic surgery has become as routine as a root canal, this expanded and updated edition of fresh and incisive commentary challenges the media's standard notions of beauty with honesty and humor.